Socially
Accepted
Volume I

By

Mordichai

ISBN: 978-0-9685699-7-9

DEDICATION

This book is dedicated to all of the social network friends, fans, fiends and followers of not just the **Mordichai Music (& everything) UniVerse**™, but of our unique bands, musicians and artists alike. It is with this weird, almost cultish fan base that we continue to produce and create not only music and moving images but still images as well.

You inspire us.

CONTENTS

ACKNOWLEDGMENTS

We acknowledge the innovative creators of the current social media platforms which have allowed us to expose ourselves publicly. As this is written there are multiple sites which have focused on being aggregates of the frenzy of photo and video as the world takes part in a global exposé.
For the purpose of this book we have focussed on one particular social media outlet – Instagram.com. So it is with great pleasure that we acknowledge them specifically, as well as ALL of the amazing followers of the @MordichaiMusic Instagram site.

Thank you.

Chapter 1
Outside Inside

We are social creatures. Even the most hidden away people wind up talking to themselves, animals or ghosts eventually.

The 21st century has brought with it technology beyond the imagination in ways which would have, and may still be, considered witchcraft. I've had many moments when we would be on the road or in the studio or wherever and it was time to post something online, and thanks to the technological wonders, I could take a photograph, edit it, and post to all of our social websites without using anything except the handy cellular phone I had at my disposal. This ease of access to technology brings us closer as a global family, connecting the cells of the hive seamlessly with microwaves, invisible to the human eye.

Not only do we get to share our creative works with the world faster and with more high definition resulting in better quality art, but we also get to see what our friends, fans, and family are up to in real time as well.

Here are a few of these images we have chosen to preserve and share in this hardcopy which made us a little more joy-filled here at the secluded **Mordichai Music (& everything) UniVerse**™ studios.

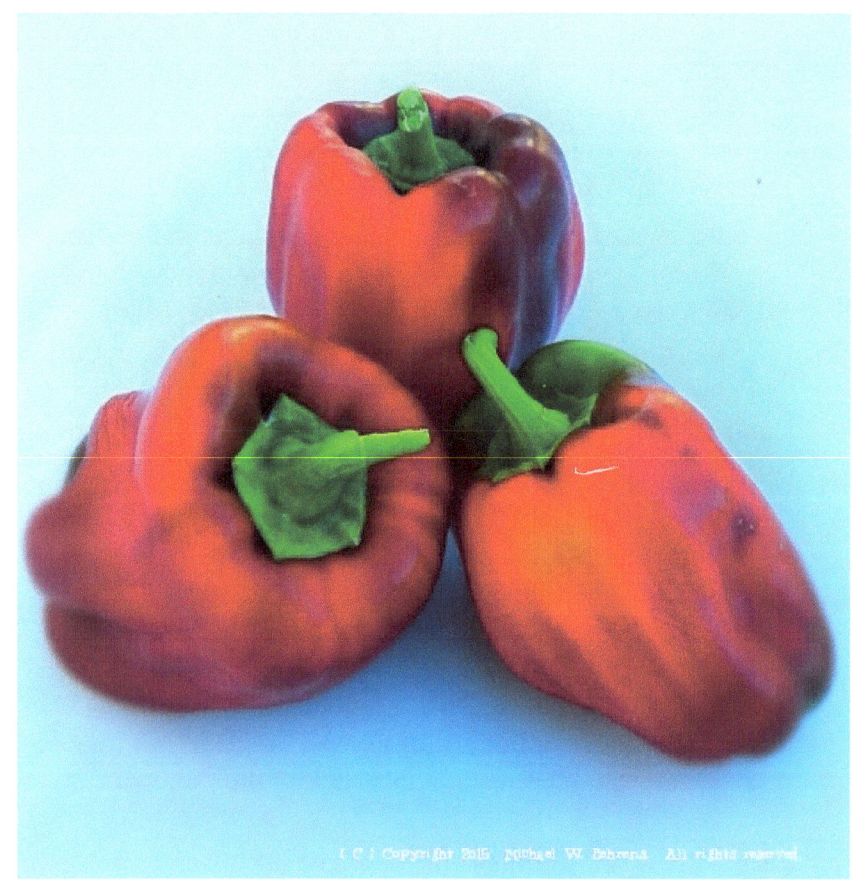

It makes for such excellent working relationships when fantastic food is added to the mix.

These peppers were started inside and grown outside the studios from seed which was procured during the preparation of a most awesome stir-fry after a very , very long day in the studio.

Months passed after the fragile seeds had been dried and pushed softly into a little bit of damp fertile soil and the green of the host plant shot up and flowered; then produced these most lovely red bell peppers in late summer of 2015.

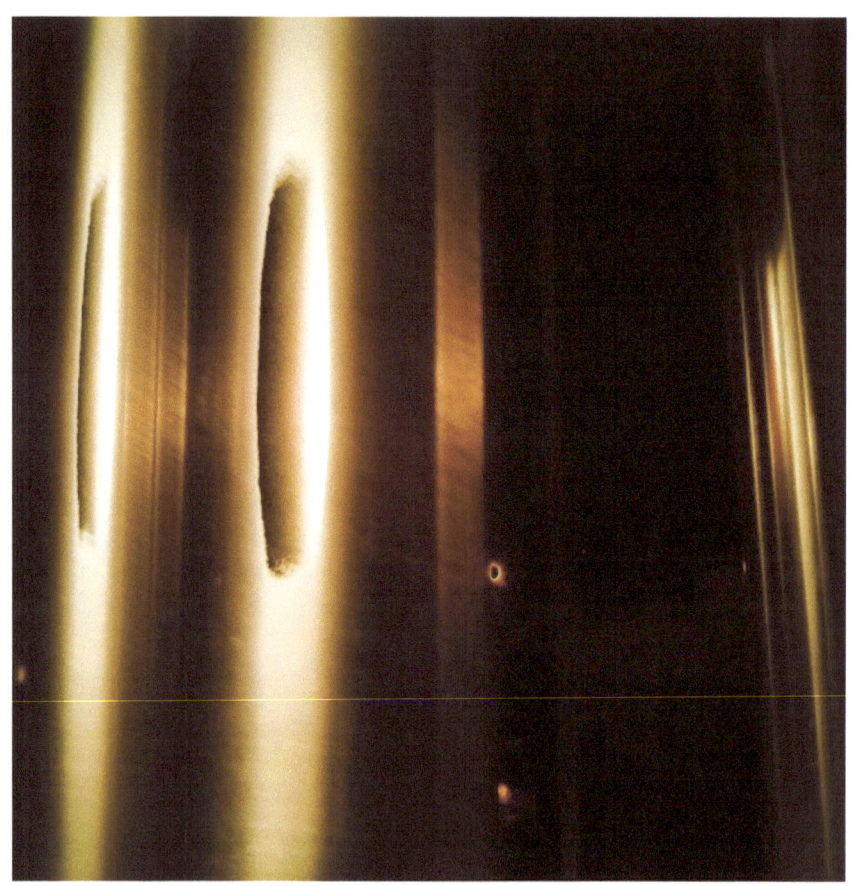

Music, organized sound. It's the foundation of magical memories both alone and with others. Even though we are surrounded by music constantly, we still sport these lovely wind chimes outside the studio doors. (No, they don't interfere with recording, not only are we sound resistant indoors, but can mute outside sounds quite effectively.)

One late night they suddenly became photogenic and this is what happened. This wasn't the first time that these musical metal tubes caught the eye of the photographer; you're likely to encounter them again before this book is through.

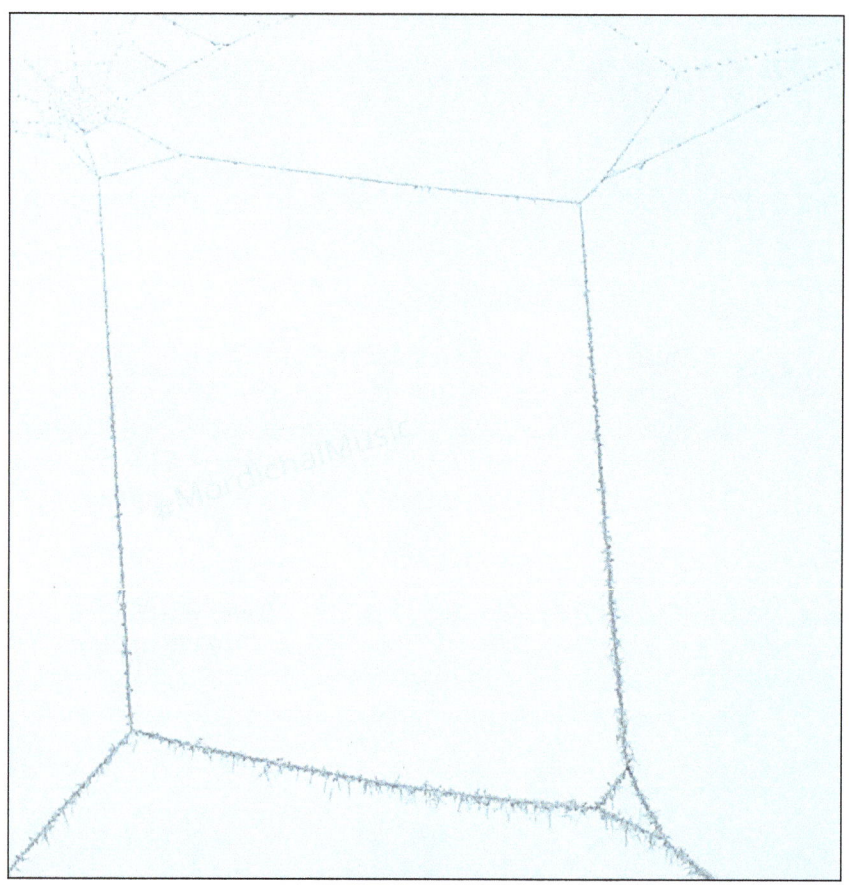

Geometric, frost glistened as the snow turned the sky a soft, weird baby blue; nearly as if someone had been using chalk pastels to paint the sky that afternoon. We like to get out of our little workspaces as often as possible as it promotes creativity from all staff around here, not just those already thought to have a monopoly on creative flow. Nonetheless we've walked outside for too many reasons to count, but always have we found the coolest little curiosities.

Did you know, for instance, that a wasp will descend upon a popcorn spider whilst the spider patiently (one assumes) for its next meal from the comforts of its own intricately planned, engineered and built, home. We have seen such things outside the building while absorbing some vitamin D.

The fate of this web's weaver is unknown to us now that the fall has landed upon us. Although other arachnids still appear, this one has been unseen for months as far as any of us know. We thank him for the cool web which gathered frost to make this photograph.

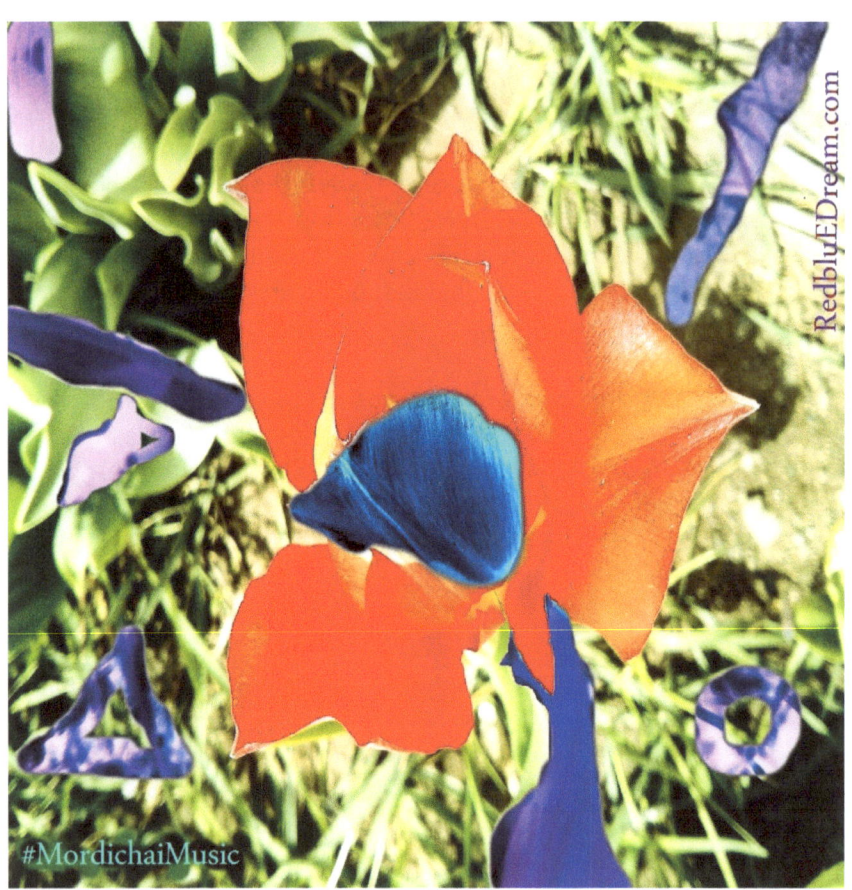

One thing we love to have around here are flowers. Lots of flowers are essential in any work space as they help clear the mind, subconsciously wiping the garbage of the moment, for a moment while you reset to a more natural, primal mode of thought. For some reason, we have accumulated several petal posts which celebrate nature and the seasons.

This is a digitally enhanced photo of one of our garden gems, not from our main studios though, this was a field trip photo from near Vancouver, British Columbia. It was found on a morning walk in a garden next to where we were staying. The red and blue enhancement was simply a creative play on our website's name RedbluEDream.com; which tends to be a bit of a running theme throughout our photographs, both raw and digitally enhanced.

MORDICHAI

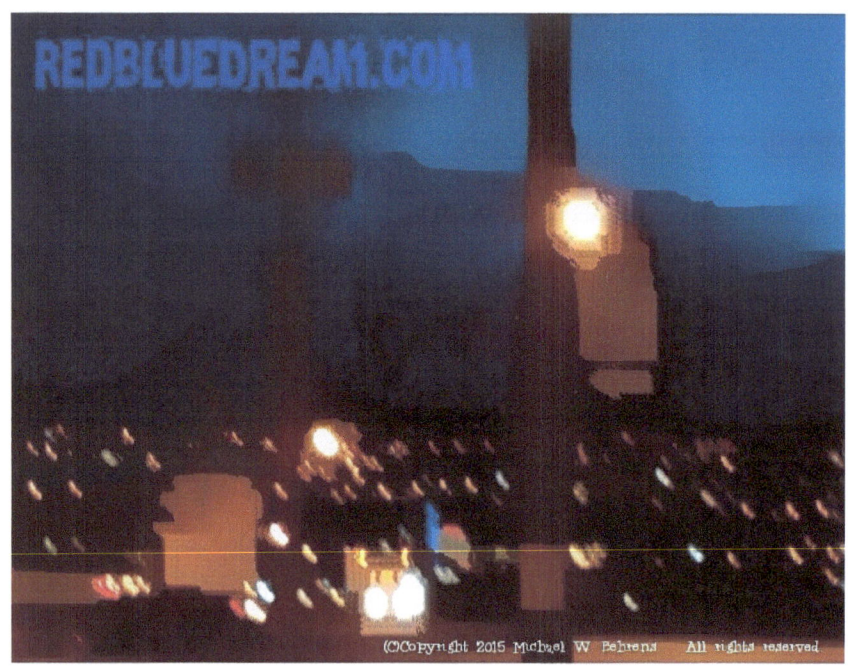

I did love the original photograph. I took the picture late one crisp winter evening in Kamloops, British Columbia. It was taken from the North Shore industrial area and overlooking the city lights.

As I said, I really enjoyed my original photograph, but I felt I could enhance it a little bit. I used a couple of programs, sometimes apps, sometimes desktop software, sometimes both or even in=camera or in-house effects such as colored fabrics over lights as filters, other materials to reflect light better and so forth.

The enhancements to this one were solely digital. I couldn't resist the soft blue and geometry of the naturally lit sky, married with the orange-yellow stippling of the street and city lights below.

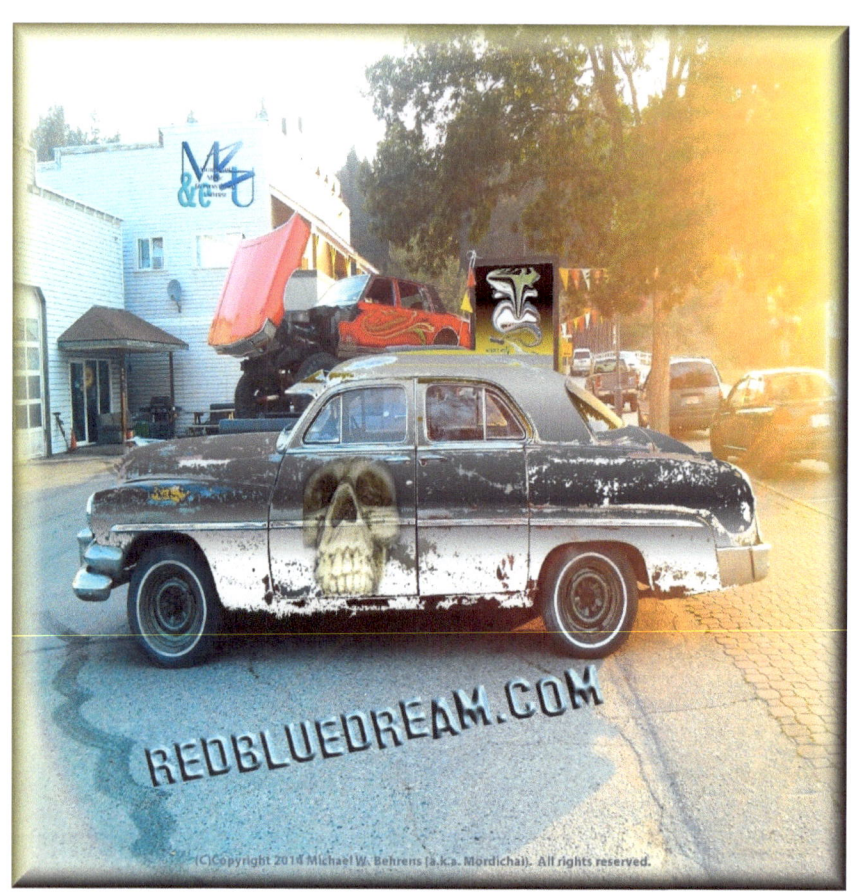

The photographer in me further wrestles with the designer and artist within in this photo taken in Princeton, British Columbia.

This is not the **Mordichai Music (& everything) UniVerse**™ facilities, nor is this one of our vehicles,. The magic of trick photography and some basic digital layering, painting and the like, transformed this car lot into a beastly makings of a horror film set.

I added the skull to the driver's door of the car in the foreground. You will see the original photograph later in this book, where we will go into more detail about the skull's origin. The driver's door on the red car in the background also had some enhancements made via a warp tool, creating psychedelic yellow swirls in the candy apple red.

On the left of the red car, the MM&eU logo appears painted on the top of the pale building. More to the center of the image there is a black and yellow mask, also a result of some warp tool work, which emulates a mask I first introduced to the mix of props and wardrobe back during the filming of one of the earlier aBSYNTh of dEATh videos.

You will also see more about said mask later.

MORDICHAI

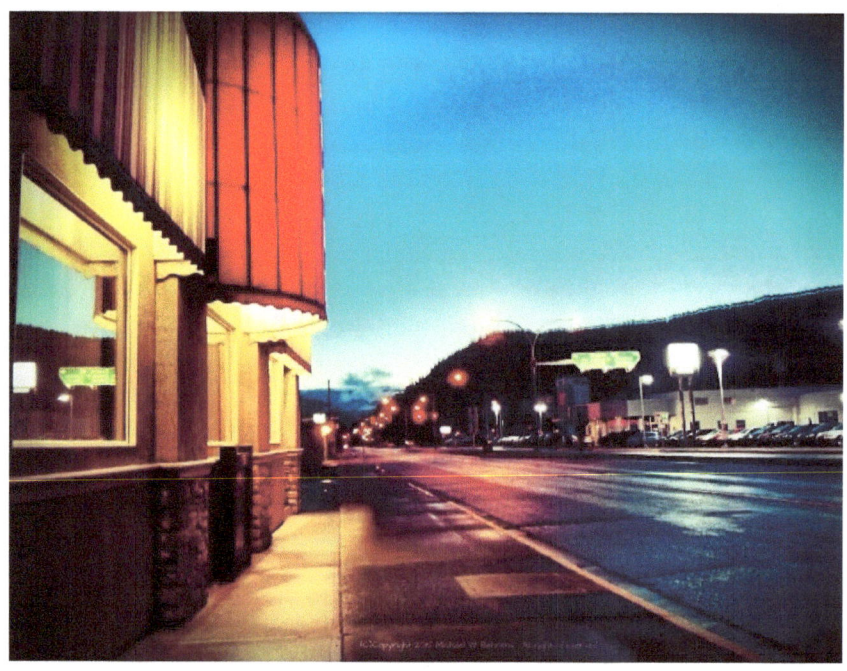

Again we see the red and blue theme emerging. This time it was moments after the sun had began to traverse across the Pacific Ocean towards Hawaii and Japan that I snapped this street shot. Highway 8 in British Columbia, blocks away from the Canadian Country Music Hall of Fame, in Canada's Country Music Capital, Merritt, British Columbia.

The evening lights were just switching on when my dusk drenched surroundings had caught my attention. The first thing I noticed was the contrast between the red canopy and the pale blue of the sky as the sun moved away from us.

The glisten from the earlier rain off the streets gave it a near metallic sheen which further made it worthy of capturing on digital film. Not much as far as enhancements on this one; simply brought out the color and contrast a wee bit.

MORDICHAI

Shadow of peace.

MORDICHAI

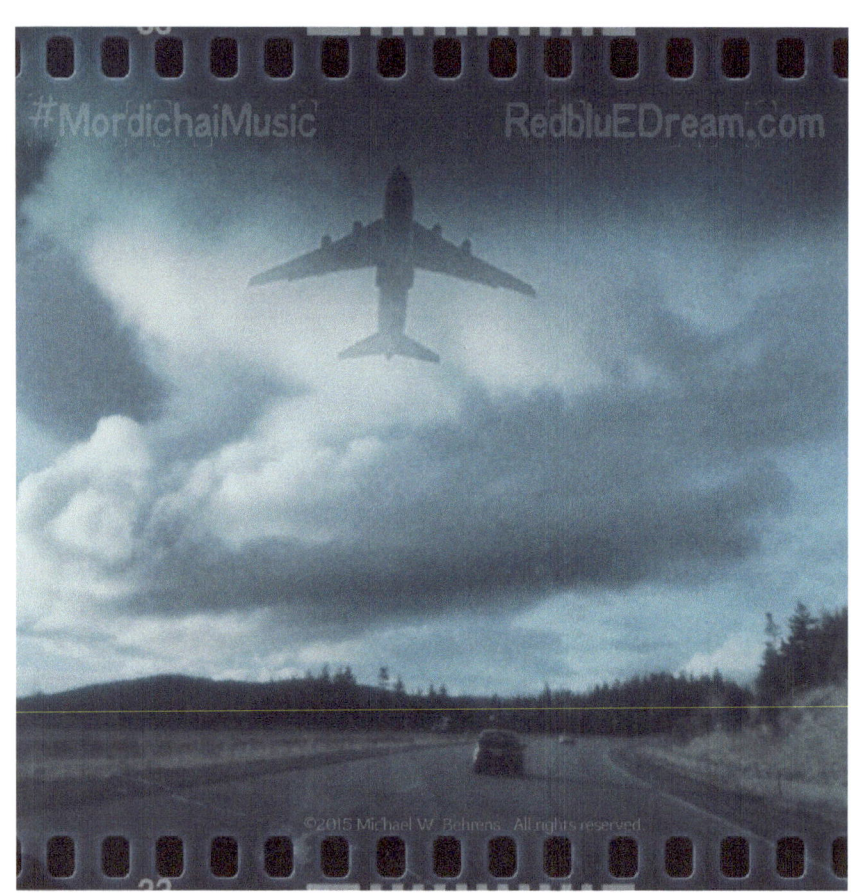

Heading east from Vancouver, Canada. The plane was photographed in Surrey, British Columbia. I am not certain whether or not any of us had noticed what airline the plane was flying with, as we were just amazed at how close we seemed to be stationed to the monster fuselages which seemed to glide effortlessly through very thin air of Canada's West Coast.

Sister Mary Phyllis, the beautiful, soft lady lead vocalist for Nina Ghostflowers, was with us on this trip and is credited with the road photo. It was the clouds she was looking at, she is always looking at clouds. Keeps looking for extraterrestrial craft; as do I, but my personal experiences will be revealed at a later date, and likely in a different format than this print medium.

The subtle blue-grey throughout the image was kind of a personal inside joke. I have a lot of those, as my art is created, it becomes like a personal journal entry which likely will not be erased. Each painting for instance, contains its own back story, as do these photographs, which really makes the creative works even more personal for me as an artist.

The images need to stand alone though. In this, one may find dark sarcastic humor of how our lives became more homogenized through technology, by the washed out blue-grey clouds, road, trees and vehicles. Alas, all art is subjective, and you dear reader are free to read nothing, or anything your heart desires from this and all images in this book of ours.

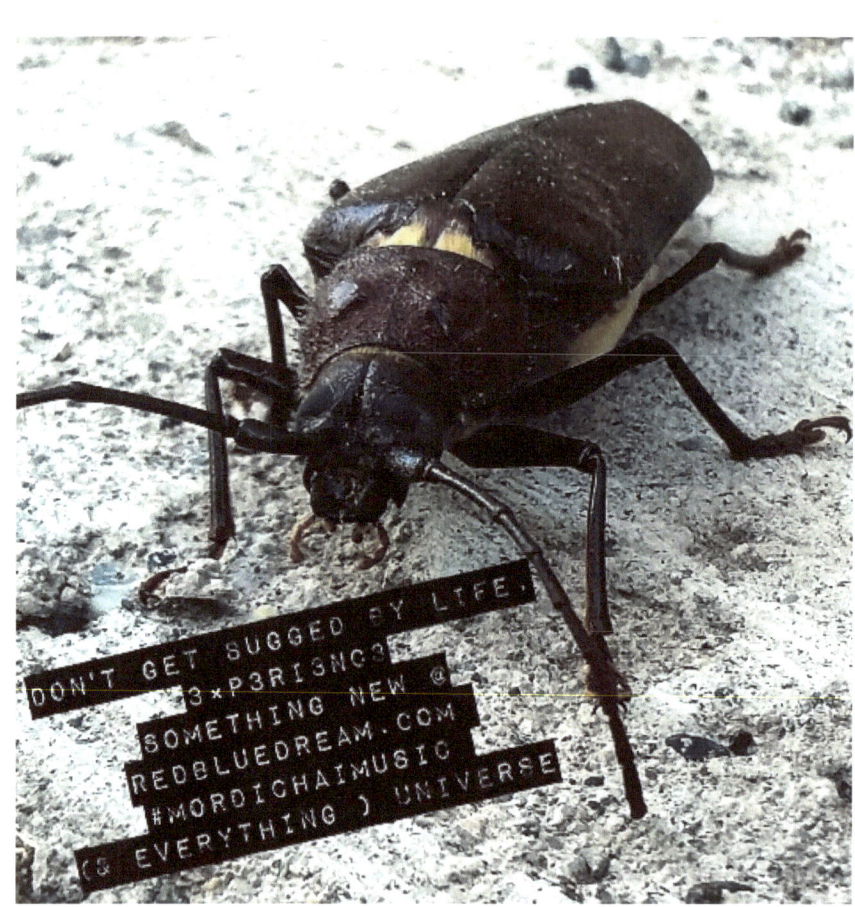

"Don't Get Bugged By Life."

This was a rescue. Again, with Sister Mary, we encountered this beetle, which incidentally was laying on its back when we were walking by. We stopped and helped to gently flip it right-side up with the assistance of three young brothers, Layton, Tristan and Brady. Funny guys.

Sister Mary and I had taken several photos of the six-legged passerby, and neither one of us is certain who took this one in particular. I do know for certain however, that I was the one who had to edit the final image. I know this because that is my quality control as the brainstem around here.

Aside from the text, there is not much of any augmentation going on in this photograph.

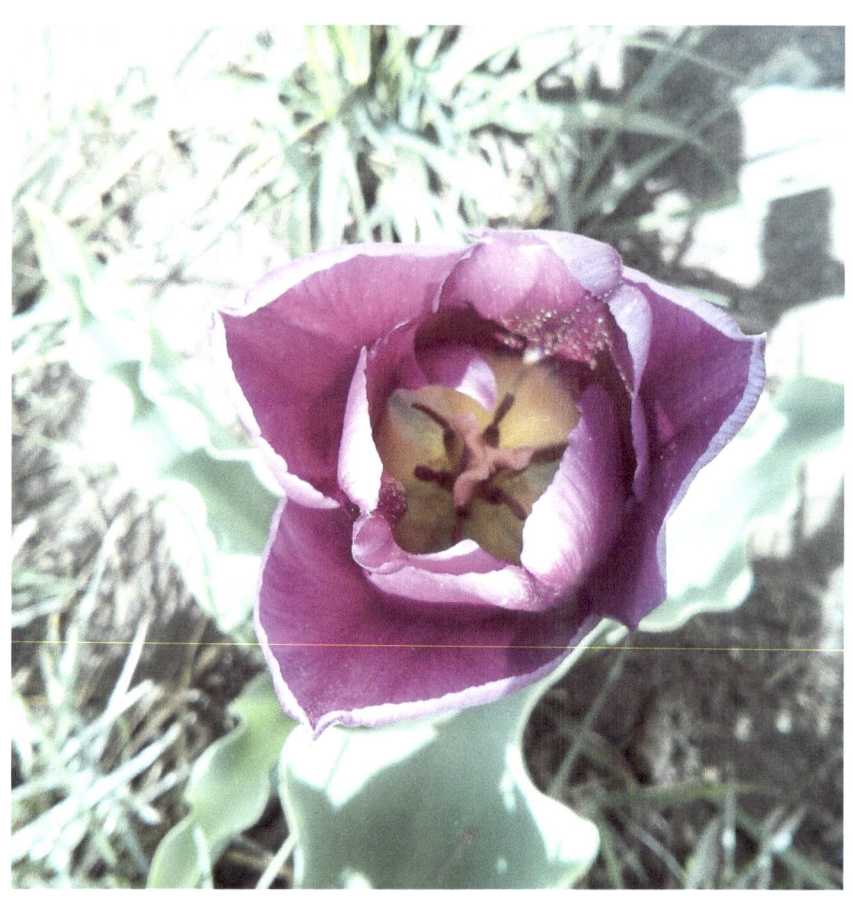

This is a tulip, slightly enhanced, but it really is purple. From our front garden in spring of 2015.

Purple and green, married nicely, the strands of grass mimicking a line drawing, and of course the yellow center of the flower which appeared as an apple sliced horizontally. These are the elements which drew me to capturing this solitary tulip.

Oh, there were others. A few of them actually, but this particular flower seemed to be wanting its solo of contrast, shadow, light and color.

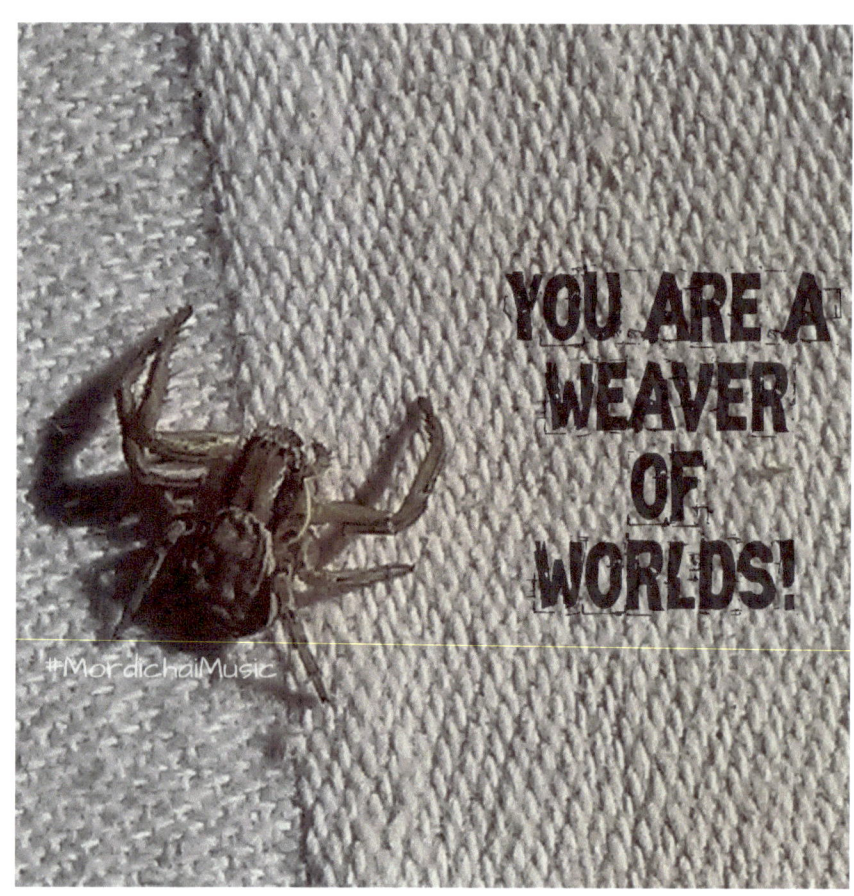

"You Are A Weaver Of Worlds"

Coming from many different cultures including first nations of North America and first peoples of Australia, basically meaning that whatever you put into life you will get back. Put negativity into the world and you get crapped on, put positivity into the world and enjoy the blessings.

This photo, aside from the text, is untouched. A tiny, strange looking arachnid was sitting on one of our outdoor pillows. So tiny the weave of the fabric could be seen on the cushion.

The lower back of the spider appears to have what looks like a mask. We like masks around here.

Good job little spider.

MORDICHAI

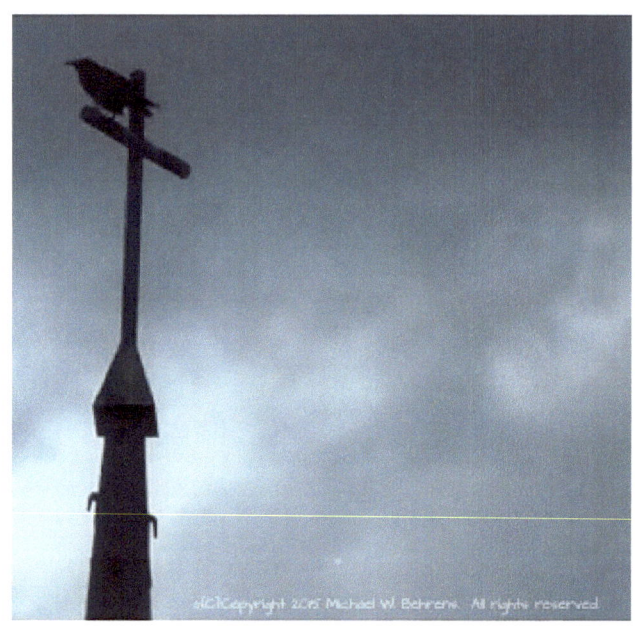

Raven on a cross against a grey sky. This moment caused me to pause and certainly take note of my surroundings.

First of all, the cross is on top of a Catholic Church not too long before the Pope visited the United States of America in 2015, and there is a raven on it. Ravens in many cultures represent tricksters, shape shifters, and messengers of ominous events to occur in the near future. That being said, if you spoke of the raven to the Arch Diocese, it would be explained to you that it is nonsense, perhaps witchcraft, superstition and so forth.

What I would really like to know though, is what the raven was thinking. Probably something like, hey that looks like a great place to relax and rest my wings in this crazy wind.

(it was a windy day)

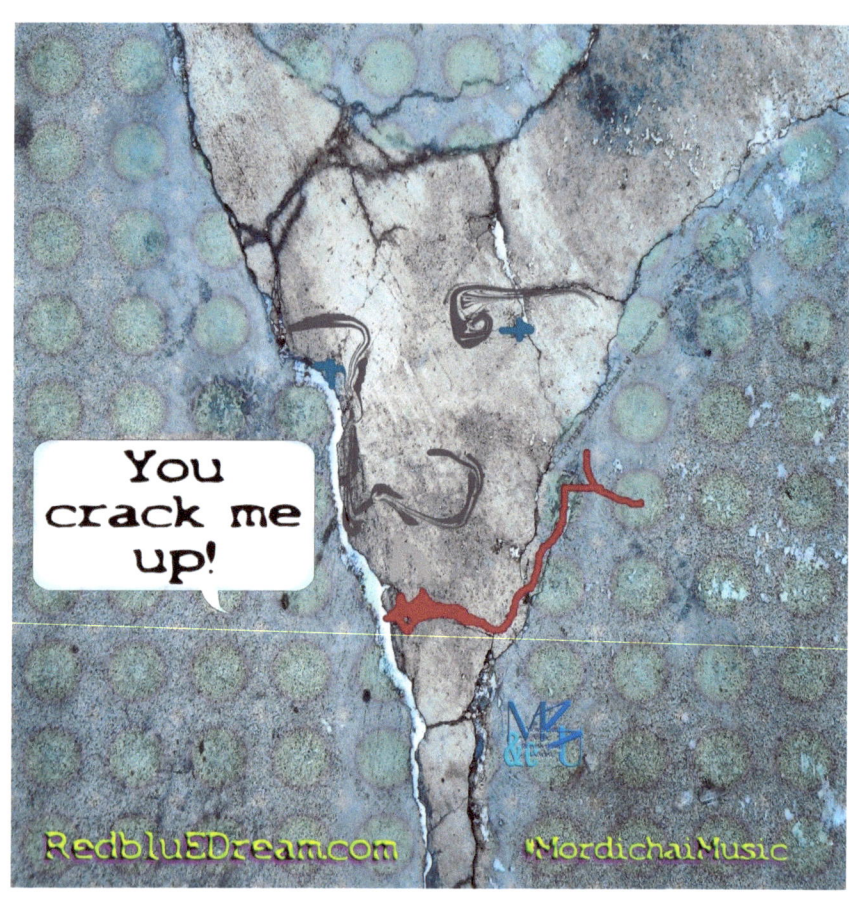

This started off as a photograph of a sidewalk while visiting a certain drummer friend. It was around the winter holiday time of year and we happened to be outside while filming a few scenes for a music video. The crack in the sidewalk just looked cartoonish to me in the moment so I snapped a shot and saved it when I got back to the computers.

* * *

The blue eyes and smile were obvious to me. I can see things on the canvas before I paint, hear things before composing and yes, I see pictures which may not be visible to others until I point them out, in concrete and other stuff.

Not high, not crazy, just can see things differently is light enough for even the most sinisterly of people to digest.

The synchronized dots surrounding the bust, balance the piece effectively for me to have my vision transferred sufficiently for the world to see.

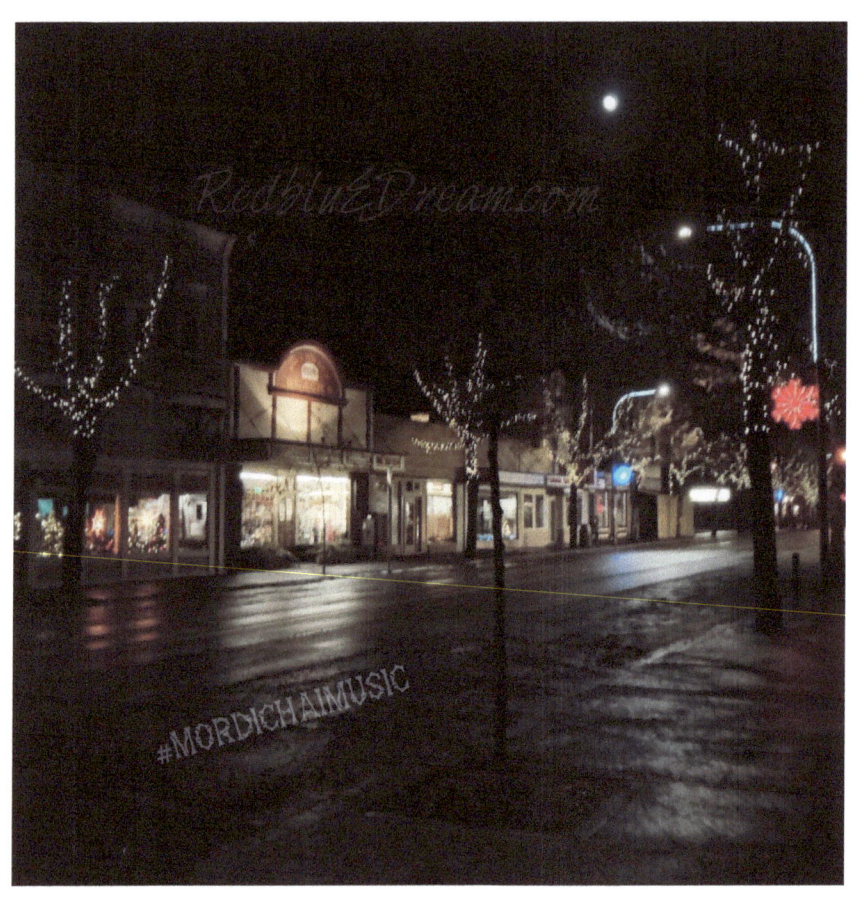

Full moon over the Canadian Country Hall of Fame.

Deserted street, wet road, Christmas lights.

A drugstore, a spa, a Freemason Hall... and Chinese Food too!

This is one of the reasons why we appreciate small towns. The quiet, the subtlety of everything and the basic idea that spending time with friends and family may not be such a bad idea after all.

This street has much history, too much for this book. I will tell you that it has an explosive history as one side of the road in a television pilot, and seen many country music stars, and fans as well.

Since there isn't usually anyone around to take pictures of the empty street, I took it upon myself to preserve the moment.

MORDICHAI

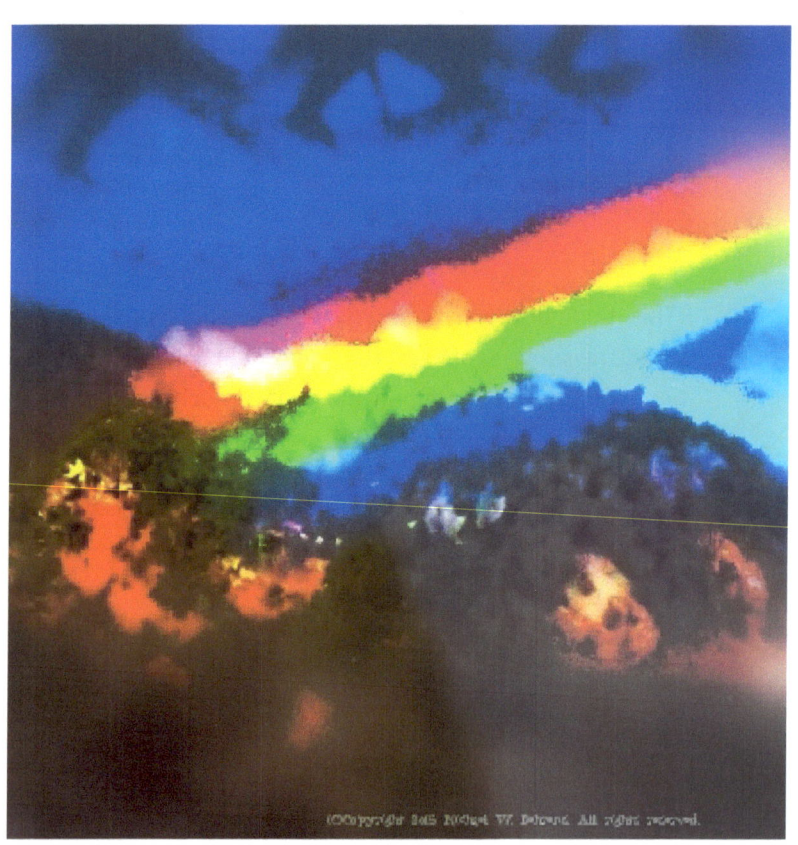

34

This is my Rastafarian rainbow. Was taking a recess, and saw a very impressive rainbow just bursting with intense color like a hologram or something. I figured it was probably just raining more heavily where I see the color. Anyway, I took several pictures, found my favorite one and began to riff on it in my favorite desktop editor.

This was my final composition, the Rasta rainbow. Colorized beyond safe limits for wedding photography, but when applied to my rainbow photo brought out the best. I also airbrushed a few details in there for added background bits of interest. Layers. Everything I do is multilayered. Has to be. Everything is.

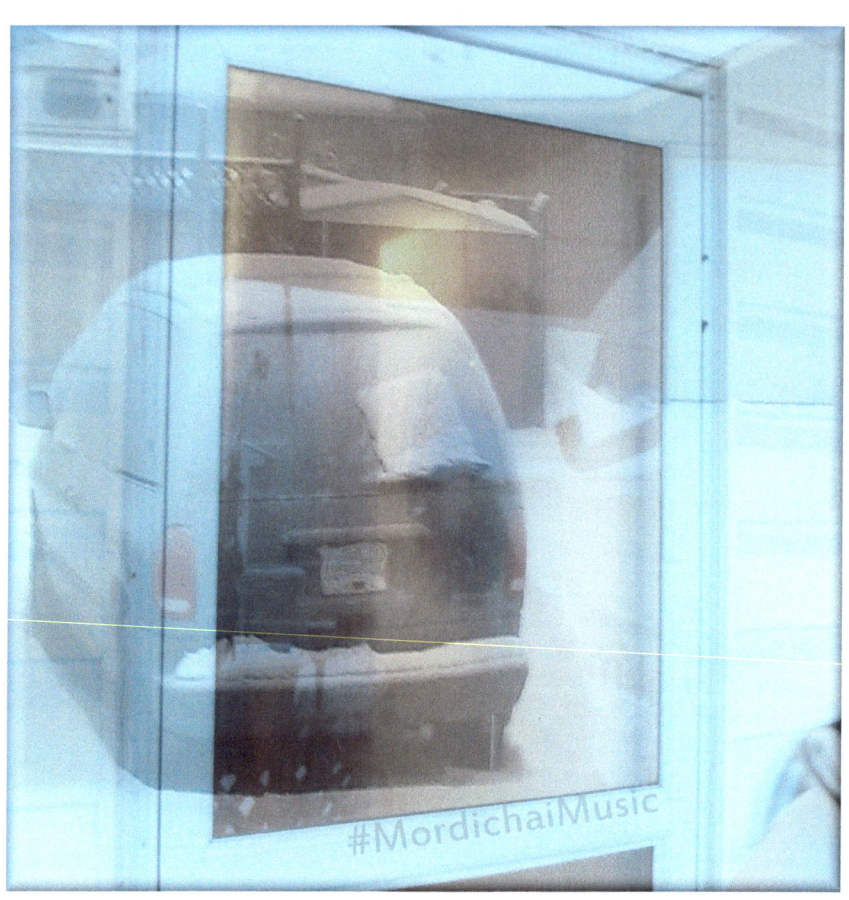

Squares. I like them. This is a little bit of an optical illusion. Two photos layered with a set opacity can bring such desired effects as this.

This is one of our non-discreet vehicles we use so as not to draw attention to ourselves, seemingly reflected off not only the outside storm window, but off of the building itself as well. Considering it was vinyl siding next to the door, this would not have been easily replicated.

I often noticed in my many comings and goings through this particular door, that if the van was parked in a certain position it appears as though it was inside the window. Naturally, I felt the need to actually demonstrate under my own controlled environment; lining up the van and the window in separate shots so they would pair up as intended. As expected it worked flawlessly, like magic.

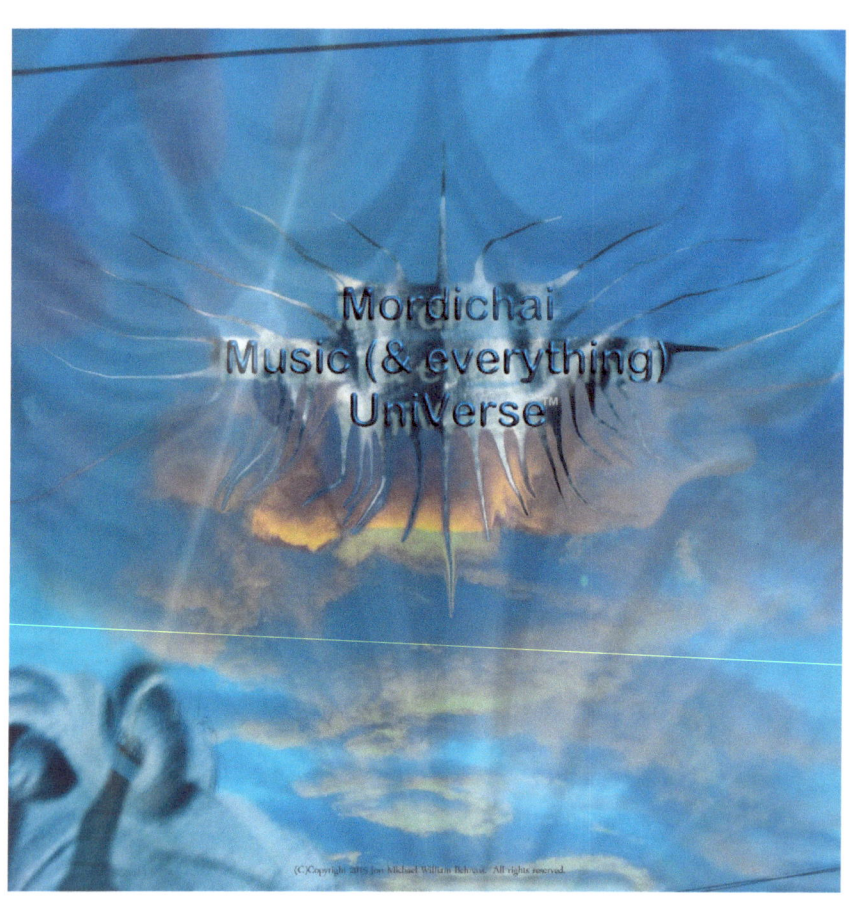

Sometimes I find it fun and fascinating to experiment with the editors. Here I was looking to emulate a painting using photographs in conjunction with some basic digital editing skills.

Sometimes simpler is better.

In this circumstance I believe I had not only attained my goal of emulating a painting with basic digital tools and photographs, but was also successful in creating the essence of a being with a giant head, looming, ghost-like, in the sky. Maybe it is a genie wearing a grand turban, or they who dwell behind the blue curtain. Perhaps it is just the Grand Wazoo, saying hello.

Note the color change, as the blues give way to purples and a yellow/orange band emerges from the third eye, capped in a crown of white. Staff heads and instrument heads dually represented in the bottom left, as a beam of white, glistens and shines from the 'M' in 'Music' coming down and reaching the staff/instrument head.

So what began as an experiment had transformed into a piece called "The Magic of Music" as it fluttered through my mind on a whim as some of the best inspired ideas seem.

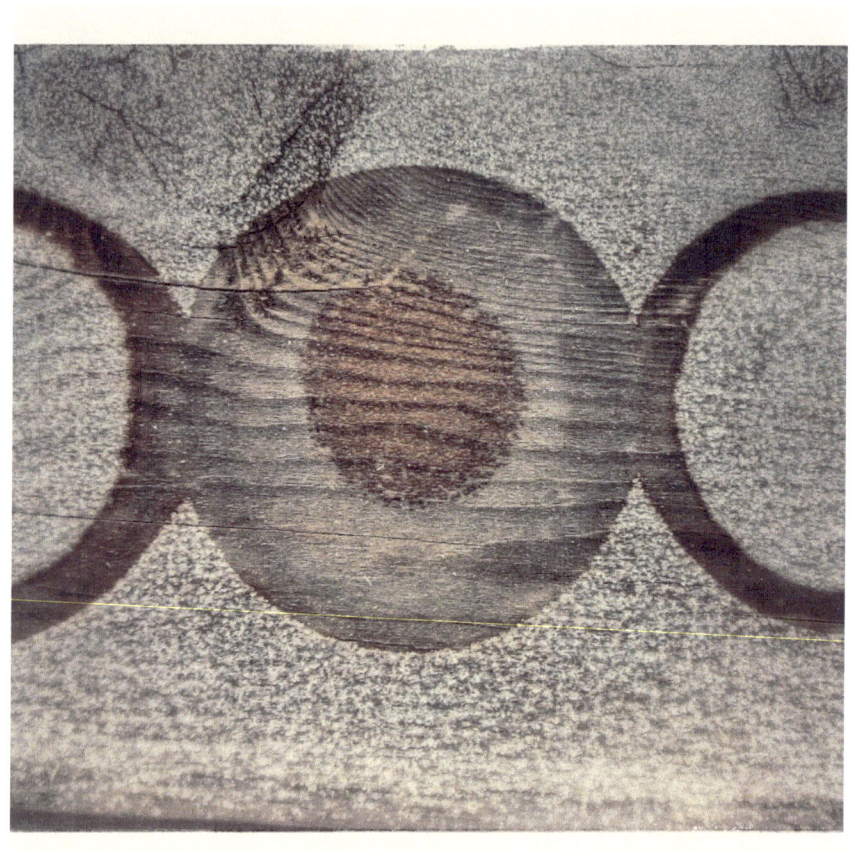

The last of this *Outside Inside* chapter is a very personal one for all of us who dwell and work and sleep and work and well, so on. It involves hot beverages, and this became a social media post by our label because many of us consume multiples of steaming hot beverages. That being said, we are workaholics who have to go outside for our fresh air recesses even in the colder days and some days are way colder than others around here.

So we put our beverage containers on the rail of the outside of this place we rented and one chilly day this became part of our morning refreshment time, and since it looks like an olive with satellite dishes for ears, one may suggest that from a slightly more abstract perspective one could perceive it as a Cyclops comet with wings hurdling right toward you. I like the olive perspective better of course. Less destructive, more tasty.

MORDICHAI

Chapter 2

Ghosts & Ghouls We Love

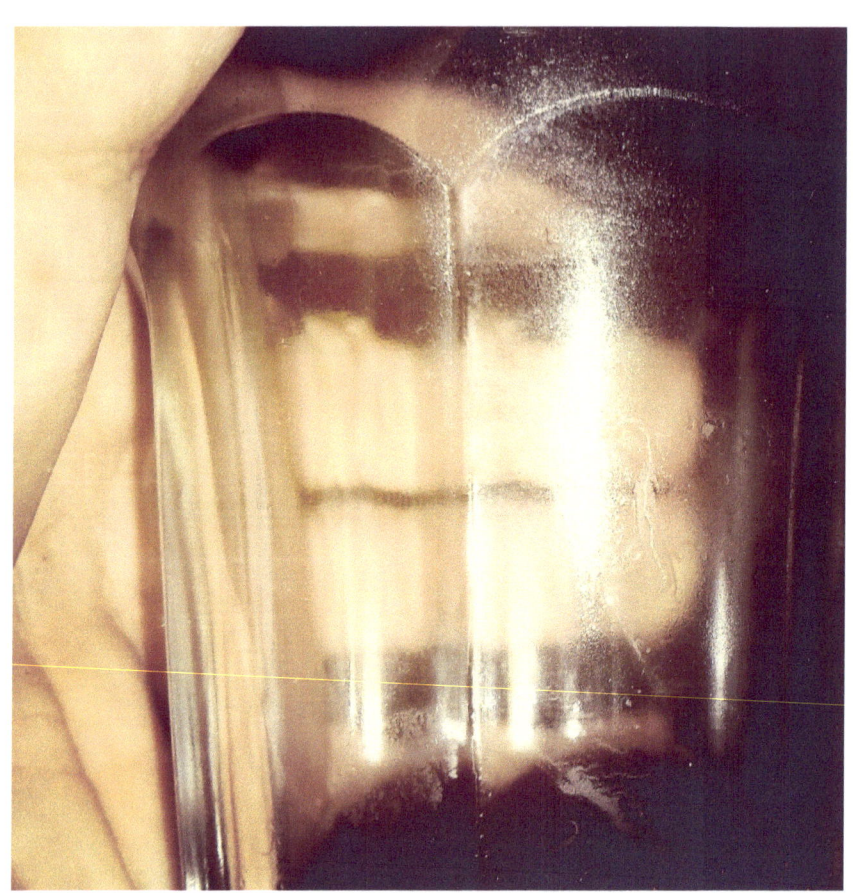

I looked down at my empty glass for some reason and saw a skull there. Now, I can hear some of you laughing because the inception of this label had been based on pretend monsters versus real monsters. And yes, for those who didn't realize that already, there are real monsters on this and other worlds. More so this one though, and since you are not accustomed to interplanetary travel as much as some, it does not mean it does not exist, I have come to learn.

We see all kinds of strange goings on around our sets and studios and this was the first time this happened, which made it noteworthy, and thus a social media post.

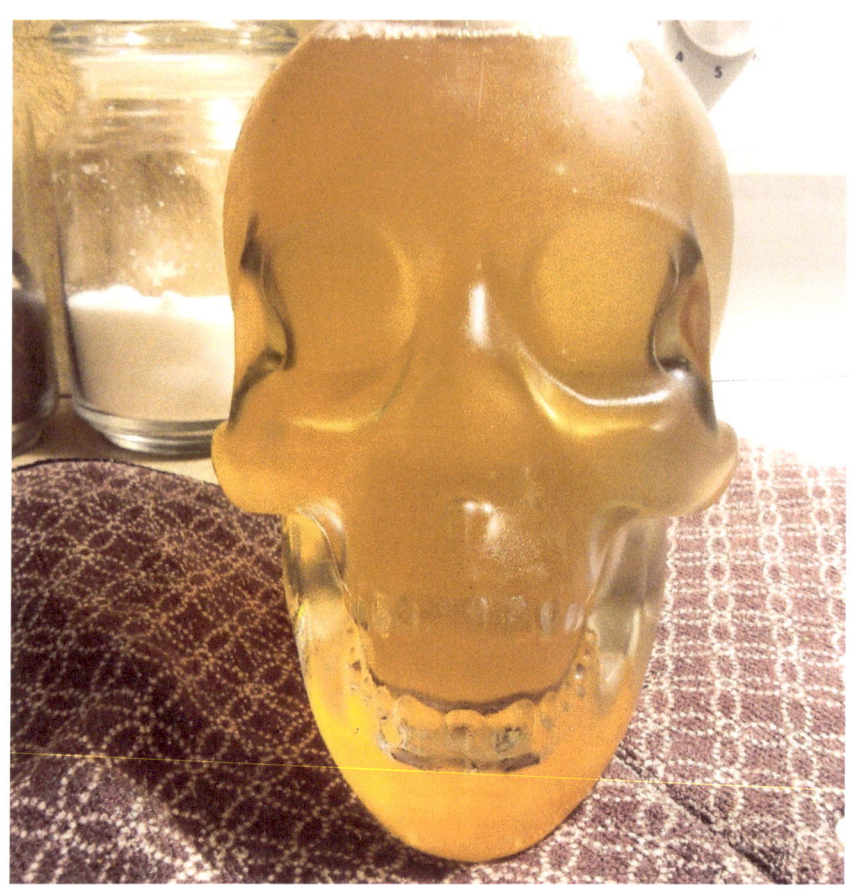

Golden Skull. This thing is a boomerang. Kept returning to our kitchen over and over and over. Usually it returned empty and would leave full. Caught a photo of the wine demon before it exited the building one night. Impressive feat considering it never usually made it more than two or three blocks from the studio before returning, as far as we know.

Current whereabouts, unknown.

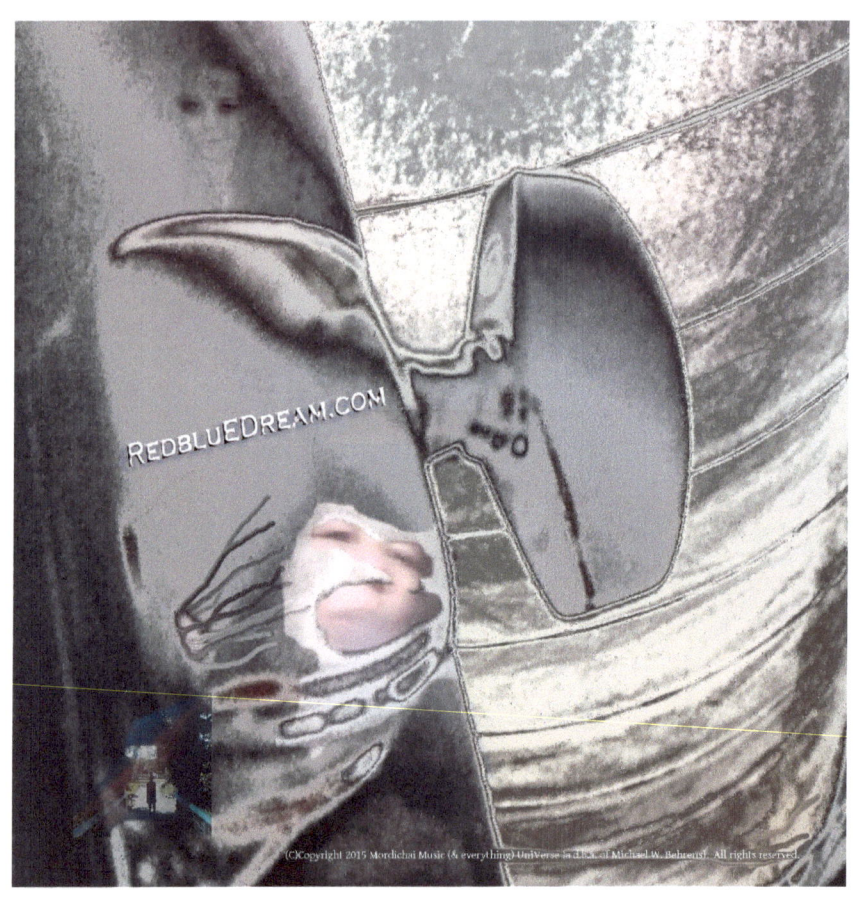

I am fascinated with reflection, glass, chrome, steel, ice, I really don't care, it amazes me how every thing merges in a world that we can't touch. Like a living 3D twin who only mimics or mocks us.

Anyway, a billion points if you can tell me what videos of ours that lamp seen in the background has been used.

In the foreground we have Sister Mary Phyllis' reflection next to the tuning peg/key. On top sporting the red and blue eyes is our twin ghost visiting while the music plays.

Sometimes it is a whirlwind of sound which brings us together as we all have a heartbeat which is our own internal music.

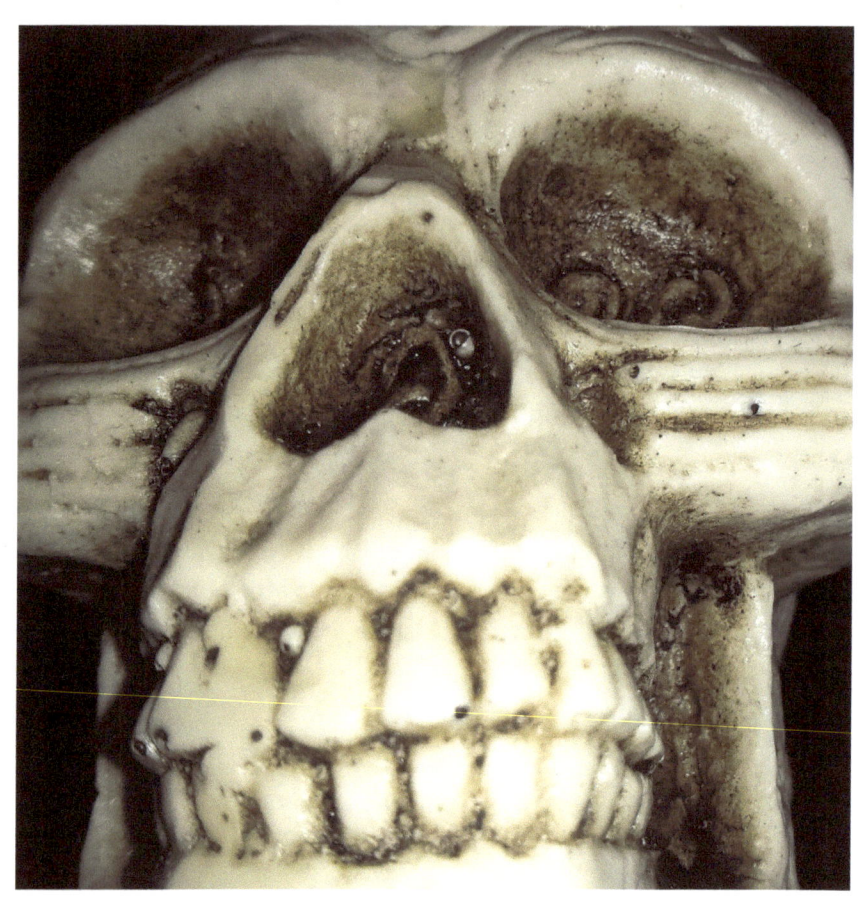

Recognize this from the Princeton, British Columbia photo earlier? This is the skull I had photographed and later re-used to plaster on the side of a car earlier in the book.

This skull is resin and came here directly from Mexico, along with tequila and that is all I will mention of its travelling buddies.

This skull just looked cool when we received it so we figured we would add it to our social media collection of images.

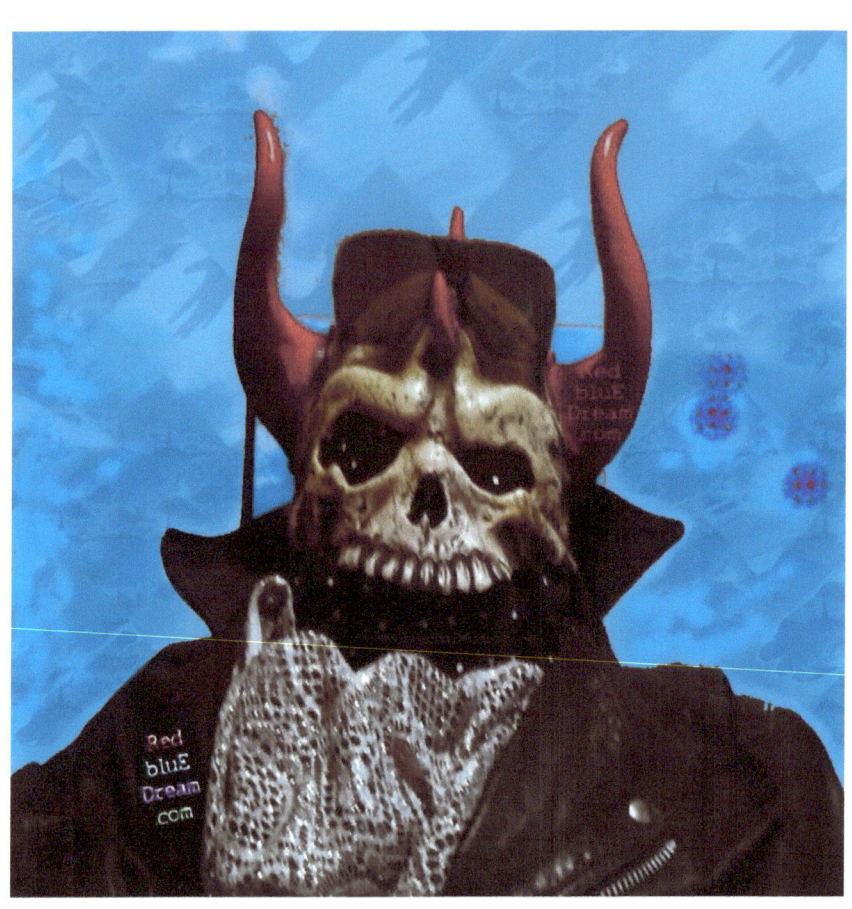

This is *Mass Cott*, for lack of a better name. He is an ever changing staple at the Mordichai Music studios. His clothes change more than some of our artists. I wish that was funnier.

Seriously though, *Mass Cott* has been the life of many parties here and thus become a bit of a celebrity himself, starring in several of our social media posts as well as being featured on hoodies and even the label's first longboard design.

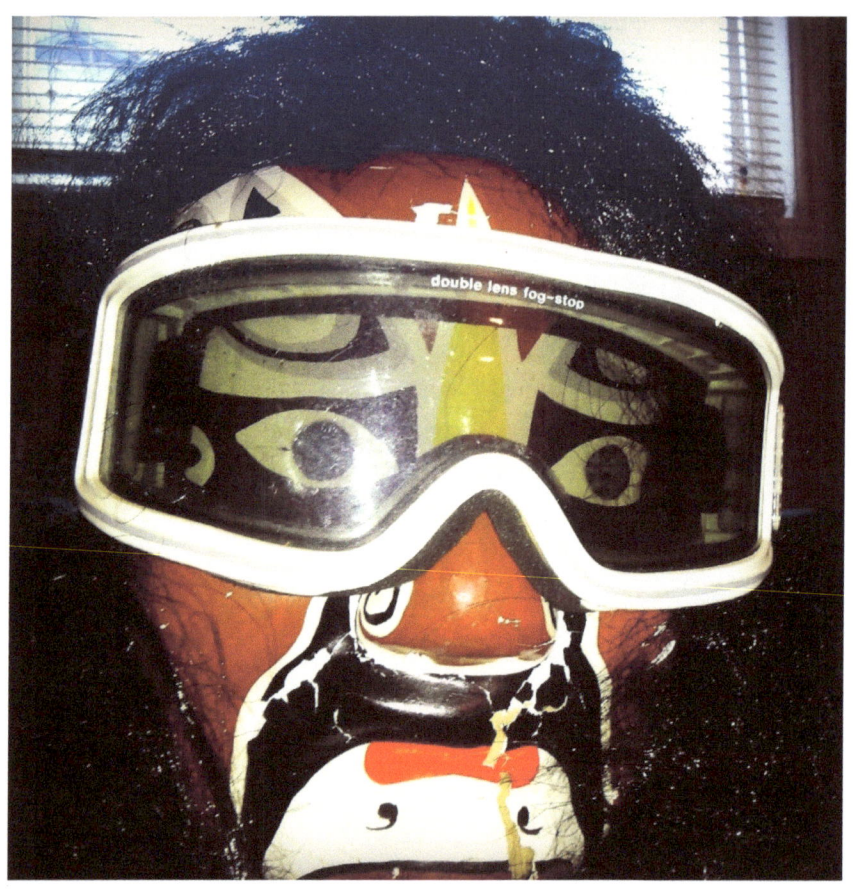

Like Mass Cott, this is another ever changing member of our studio. Bought for $5 Canadian at a community sale on the side of the road, this mask has appeared in several aBSYNTh of dEATh music videos as well as our social media, but likely best known as "Jimmy Alaska" on Facebook.

We expect this guy to continue on a lush career with us, with more music videos appearances to come.

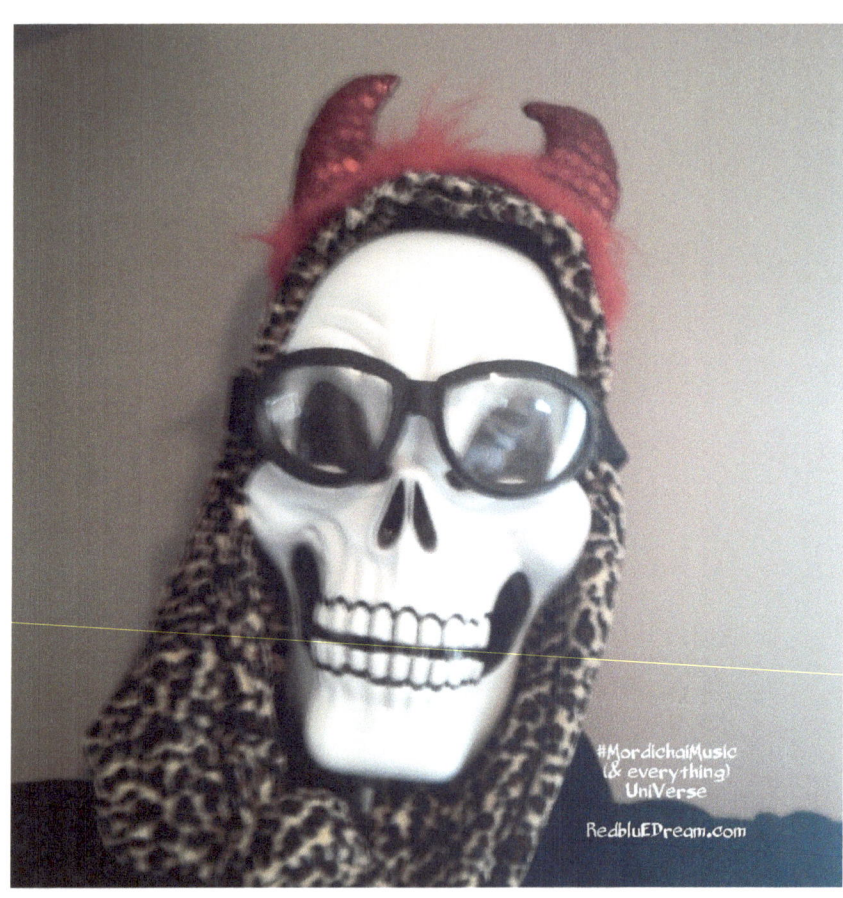

Mass Cott's alter ego.

This is a collaborative effort which required bits and pieces of wardrobe from multiple sources, and included vintage costumes from some of our dearest people's Halloween chests.

For instance the goggles came from one of the "Bootlegs For Baccaus" music video *cameo* actors and the mask and animal print 'scarf' (really children's leotards) came from a brother and sister, one of whom not only appeared on the cover of a couple albums I have produced, but also ghost writes a bit for us.

We appreciate it.

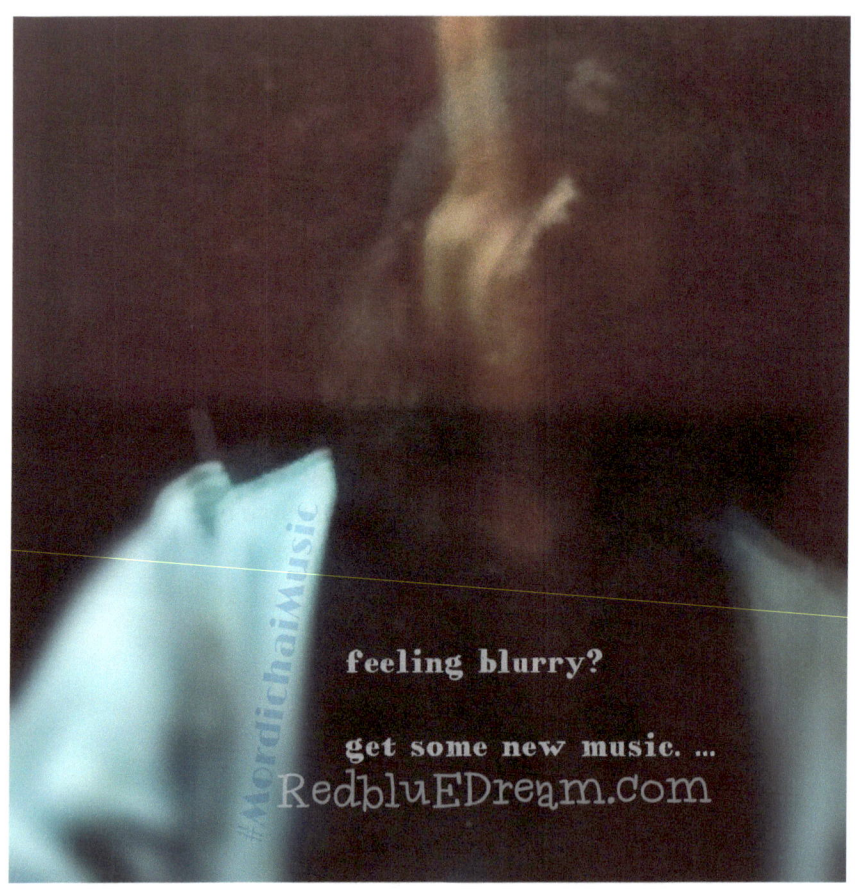

'feeling blurry?'

Every so often some of our staff have to kidnap me and drag me from the comforts of my creative playground. This was one of those nights.

However, I don't ever really stop working and saw the opportunity to take a self portrait from the reflection of the window of the establishment we had visited that evening. One of them anyway. It was a weird night as most are around our little world.

Not much as far as digital effects in this one as the lighting and dirty window lent themselves to the best of filters any artist could hope for.

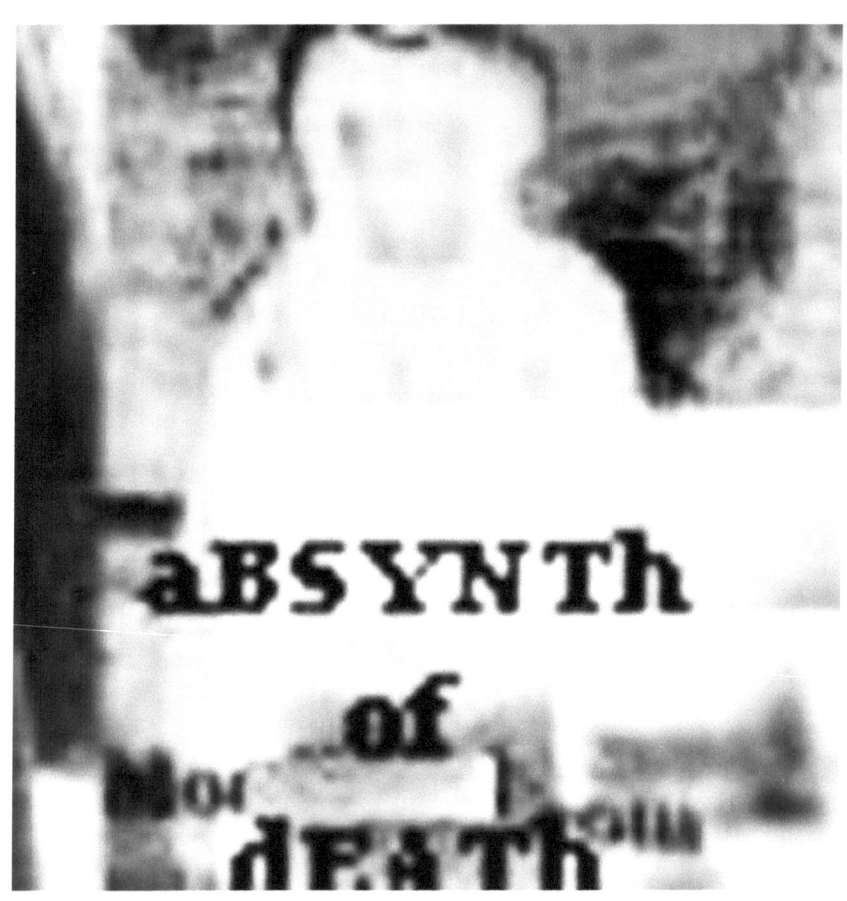

This is probably one of the oldest of our social media posts.

The stem for this photograph was taken on an old SLR camera and then digitized to be used in one of our original test websites. Now it has been seen everywhere from CBC Radio 3's website to Instagram.com.

The hat I am wearing is actually a fuzzy purple cowboy hat I had purchased at a street mall, and used while DJing throughout British Columbia.

MORDICHAI

Chapter 3

The Natural Path

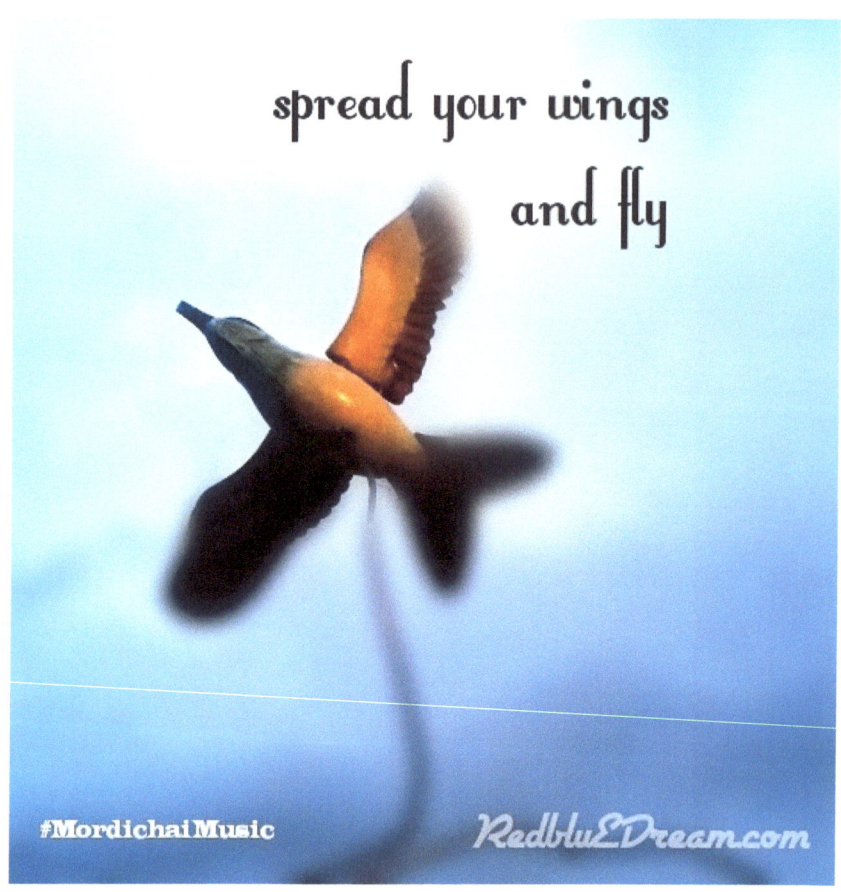

Let the 'Natural Path' chapter begin with a positive post.

"spread your wings and fly"

This is an ornament which had been given to Sister Mary Phyllis by a dear friend who incidentally has the same name as another dear friend in another town who has one of these same birds.

It appeared to take flight one lovely morning during some refreshments outdoors. Another irresistible photo opportunity had befallen me and yes I did soften the focus around the edges a bit to smooth out the incidentals.

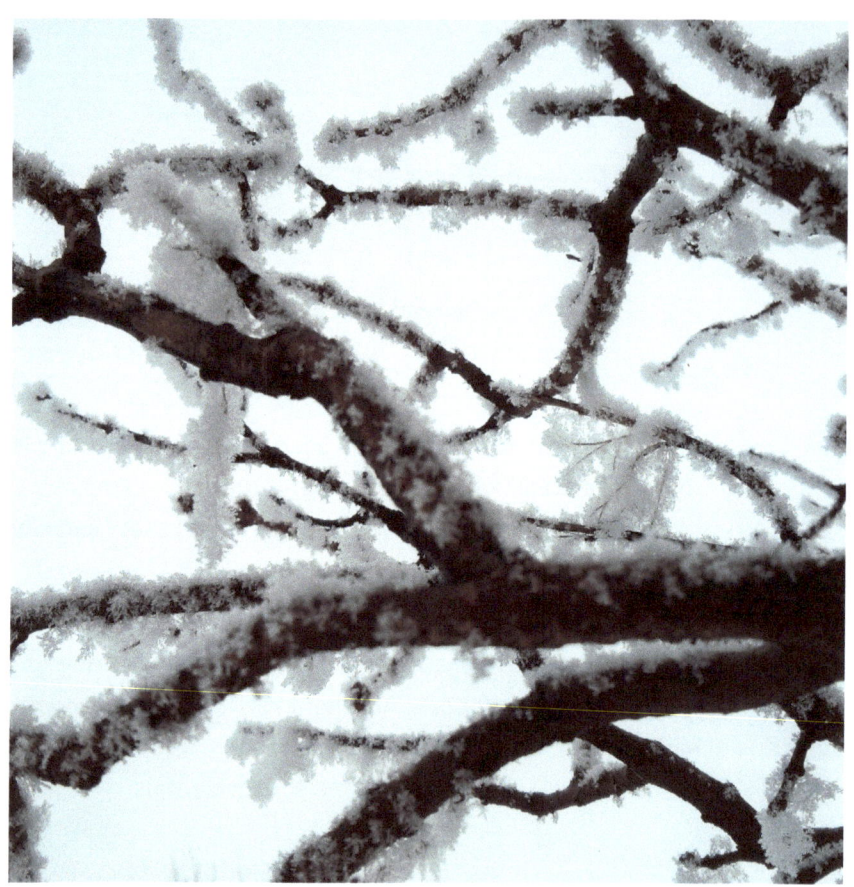

Such a lovely frosty morning this was. The crystals glistened off of everything and these little branches not too far from our usual digs a the time, just wanted to be captured in time, in that moment.

The nearby tree had lost its leaves not too long before this moment, and the grey clouds moved in and set forth their blanket of snow to cover the trees and dwellings and all that dwells in the little valley we have spent years working in.

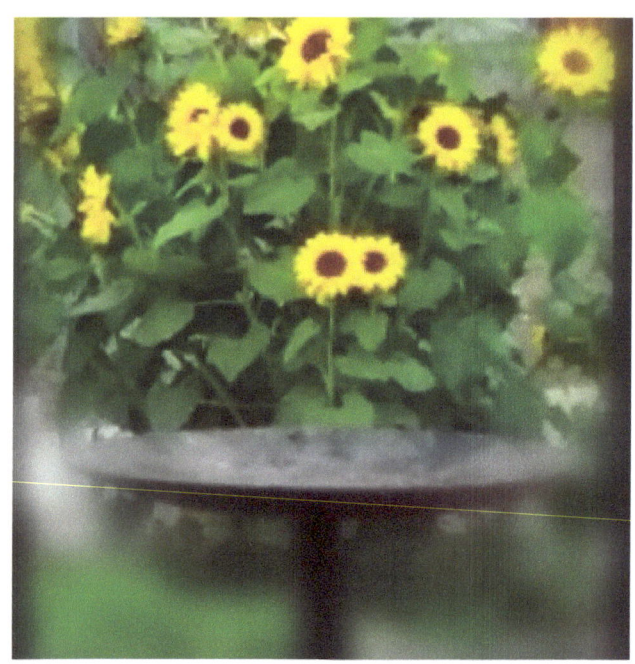

Sunflowers and an outdoor candleholder steal the scene in this photograph. This was a planned image. Potentially planned is a better statement actually. I had waited months for this lovely sunflower to blossom, just praying and hoping that it would frame itself most lovely in the center of this squared iron candleholder.

When the day finally came the light was not exactly as planned, but seeing as I wanted to get the shot as naturally as possible , I moved the iron 'frame' slightly to the right just to get the perfect shot.

I really enjoy these types of moments as the flowers were volunteers in a gravel part of a parking area behind our facilities. A previous resident had grown a vegetable garden, complete with multi-headed sunflowers to keep the birds off of her produce and these just happened to seed itself in hard-packed gravel and grow quite magnificently.

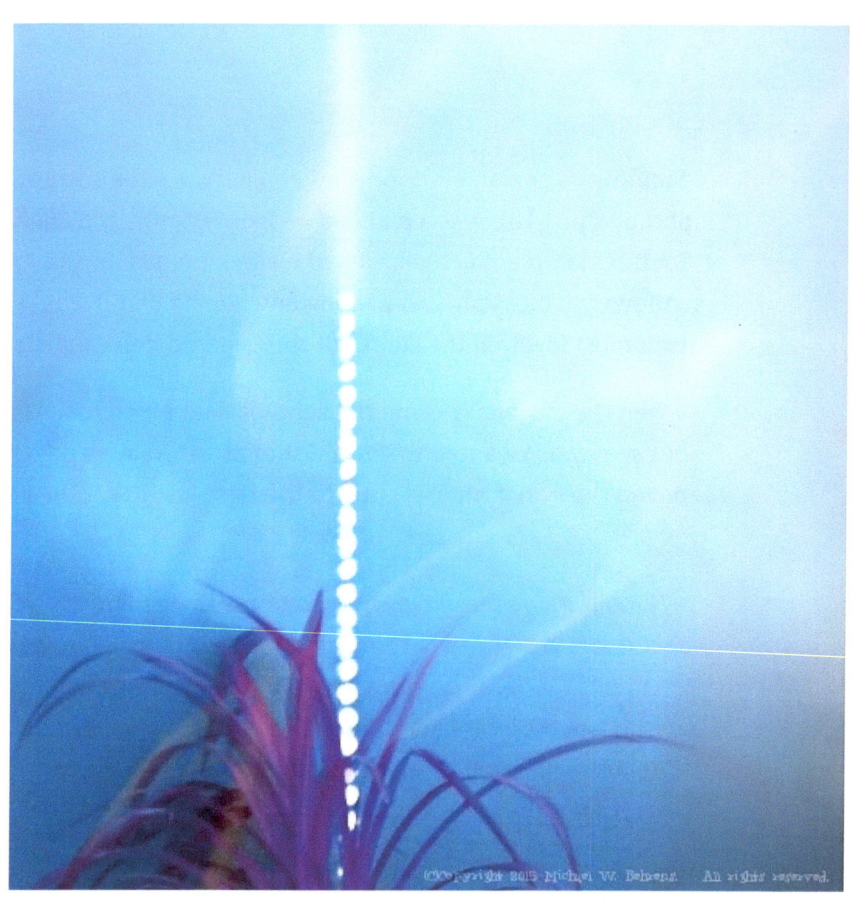

Natural sunlight streaming through some wholes in a blind in a common room window and near braised itself onto a young spider plant.

I believe this light had interrupted lunch to suggest it pose for a shot.

The greens melted into purple in the light, and the walls were certainly not blue, but it all managed to complete itself in this form. Little teasing and tweaking of the colors and hues, contrast and light and poof! We have a new snippet of a new world.

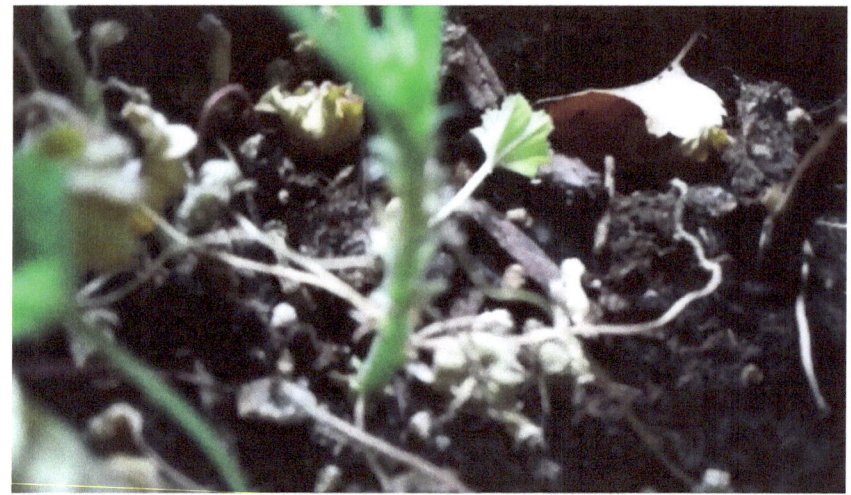

Another volunteer. Again, seems to be a reoccurring theme, this volunteer thing. Anyway, this is a little tiny plant which seemed to pop out of a little bit of dirt we had in a pot that was trying to house a pepper plant.

We loved the lush new green as it sprouted from the pot.

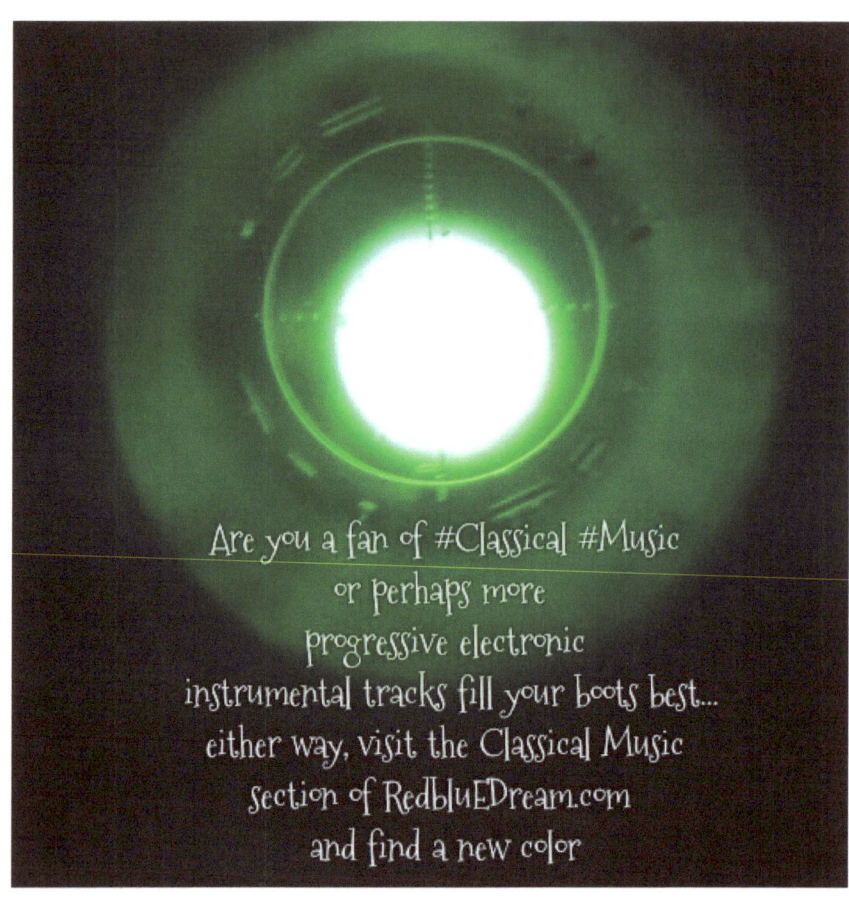

Are you a fan of #Classical #Music
or perhaps more
progressive electronic
instrumental tracks fill your boots best...
either way, visit the Classical Music
section of RedbluEDream.com
and find a new color

This image was actually a fail and not a perfect shot as I seem to be obsessed with finding.

I was using a very expensive microscope and was trying to capture the slide of an asbestos sample for one of my projects when I got this misfire. Well it wasn't so much a misfire as it was an unintentional blessing. The result of my mistake turned out just as awesome as I had intended, but just not as I intended.

The natural aspect of this shot is missing but was intended, but the finished product worked out nonetheless for another project. Just saying there is such thing as 'happy accidents.'

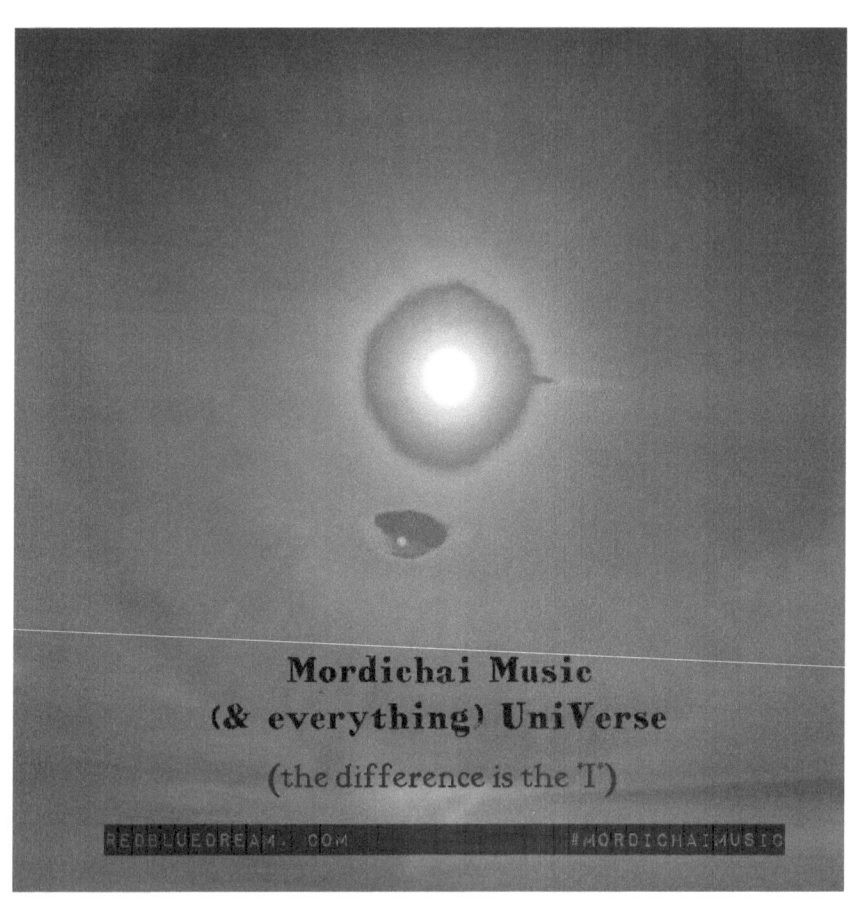

I have always loved in-camera effects better than digital. The challenge is greater and sometimes smoke and mirrors are required. I even use stage magic effects to pull of some shots, mostly motion pictures, but still photos as well.

In this circumstance, it was the standard Nexus 4 camera providing the pinkish cube lens flare design. The intensity of the sun burned into the photograph and helped to bring out the central ring. It was the huge 'Sun Doggy' circle I was attempting to fit into the picture when I captured the image.

Near the bottom of the photograph, a wisp of cloud subtly veils a mountain, revealing how low in the sky the sun had been in that moment. Winter months in the mountains means little or no sun, so we have to capture what we can, and in this case, share with the world.

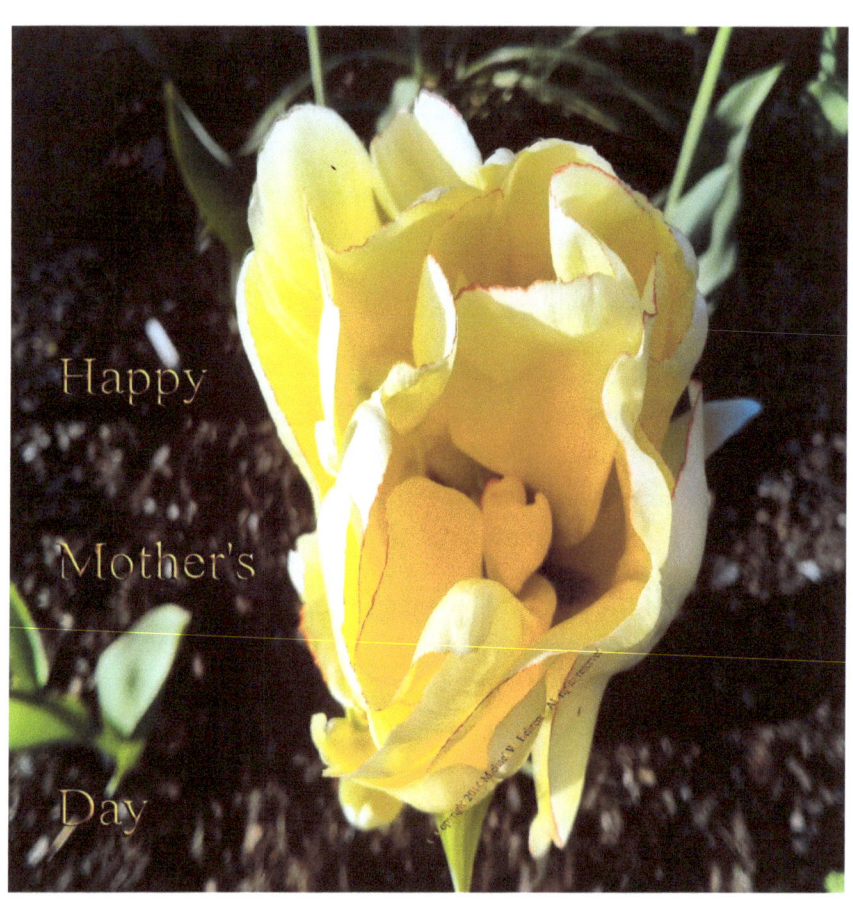

Happy Mother's Day

Since most of us have mothers, this simple yellow flower became a 'Mother's Day' post.,

We do not always have posts which celebrate specific dates necessarily.

There are many of them out there, and we feel no need to further inundate the world wide web with our well wishes.

The shape of the growing flower petals had made this post interesting enough to post.

CHAPTER 4
POP ART
(THANKS ANDY)

Gratitude to the very strange but equally beautiful world of artists like Andy Warhol and his notoriously creative gang or artists, models, musicians and curious people. We here at Mordichai Music appreciate the predecessors who have set the proverbial stage for our best digital and photographic expressions designed initially to be shared on social media outlets.

The crux of the biscuit is that we have taken our inspiration from the masters of pop art, and sometimes it shows more than others.

Without further adieu...

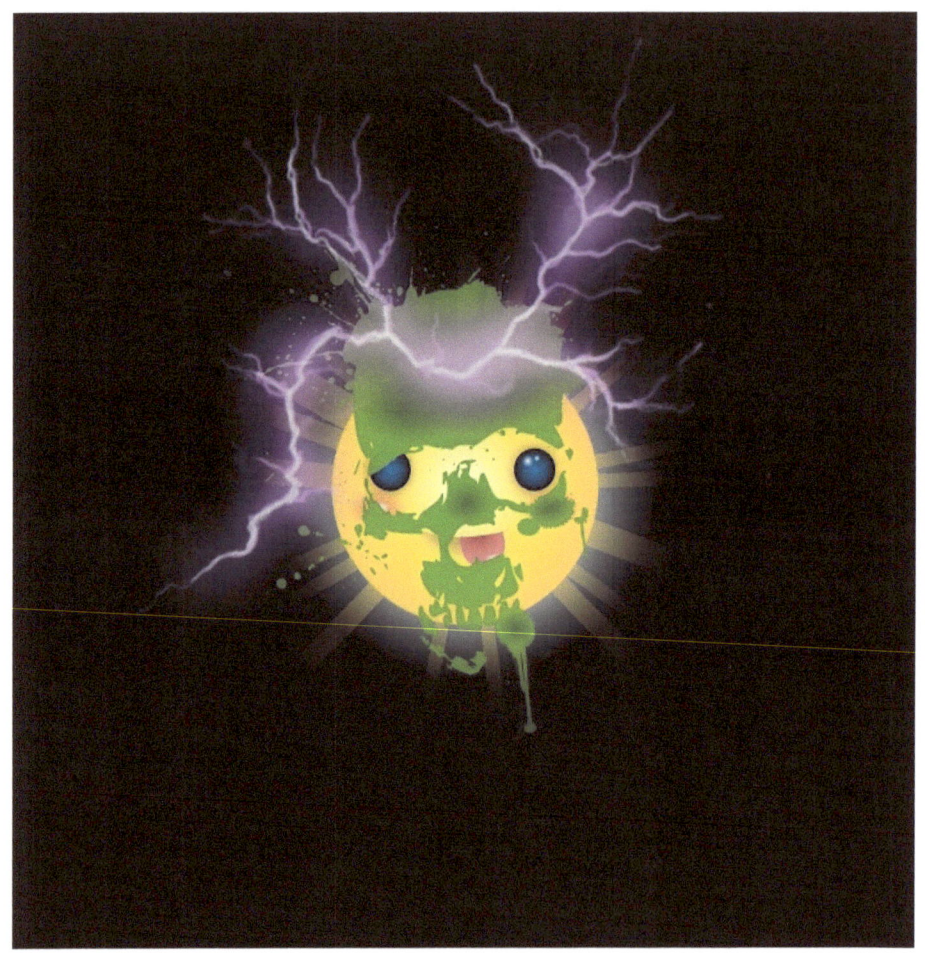

We find the need to hide ourselves behind masks from time to time. Those of us fortunate enough to know when we had inadvertently donned another personae can promptly remove them as noticed. Sometimes however some people choose to ignore their falsities with which they try to fool colleagues, friends and family.

Occasionally these masks are ugly and obvious. These obvious masks had inspired this whimsical emoji-based mask art.

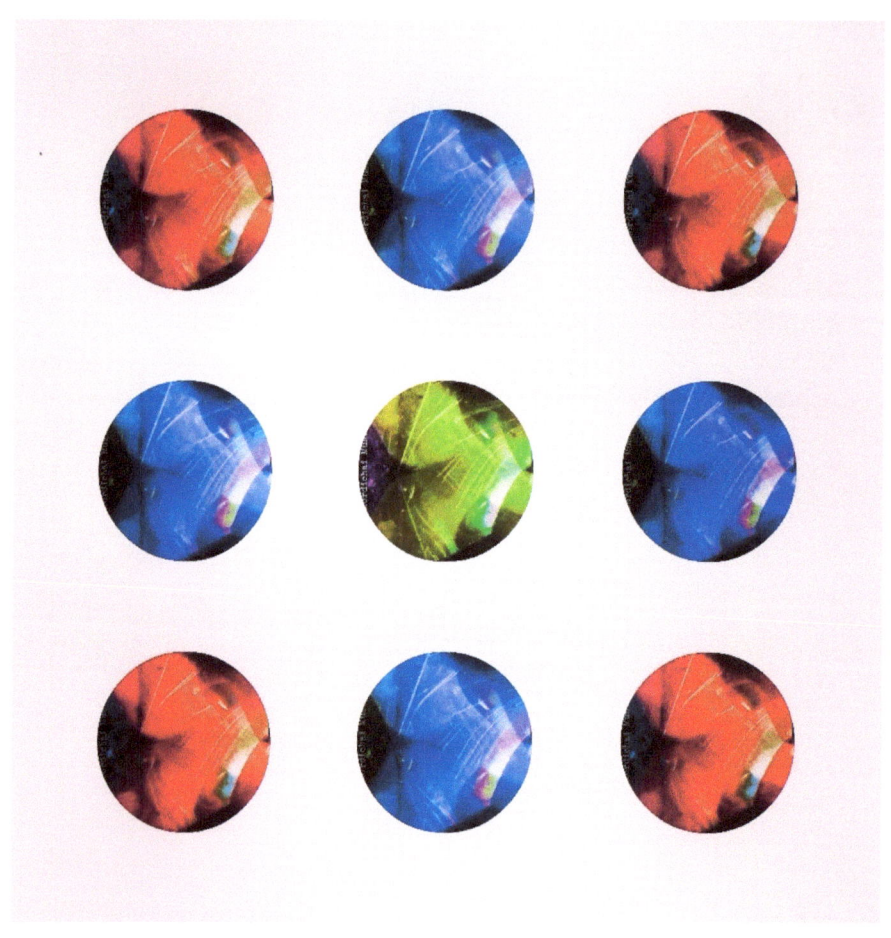

These balls are celebratory around the studio.

The original image may be revealed eventually, but for now let's just say we have had it around here for about a decade and it has served us very well. It had a luminosity one night which defied description and just begged to be photographed.

An illuminated translucent green object did gleam it seemed in the midnight light one autumn night. Things like that amuse us for some apparent reason. It could be that when we were on the Island way back when, that many in our complex had a very similar object to this.

Was a beautiful facility from which to watch a sunset in July indeed! And maybe that may have something to do with all the nostalgia attached to this so far, un-named object.

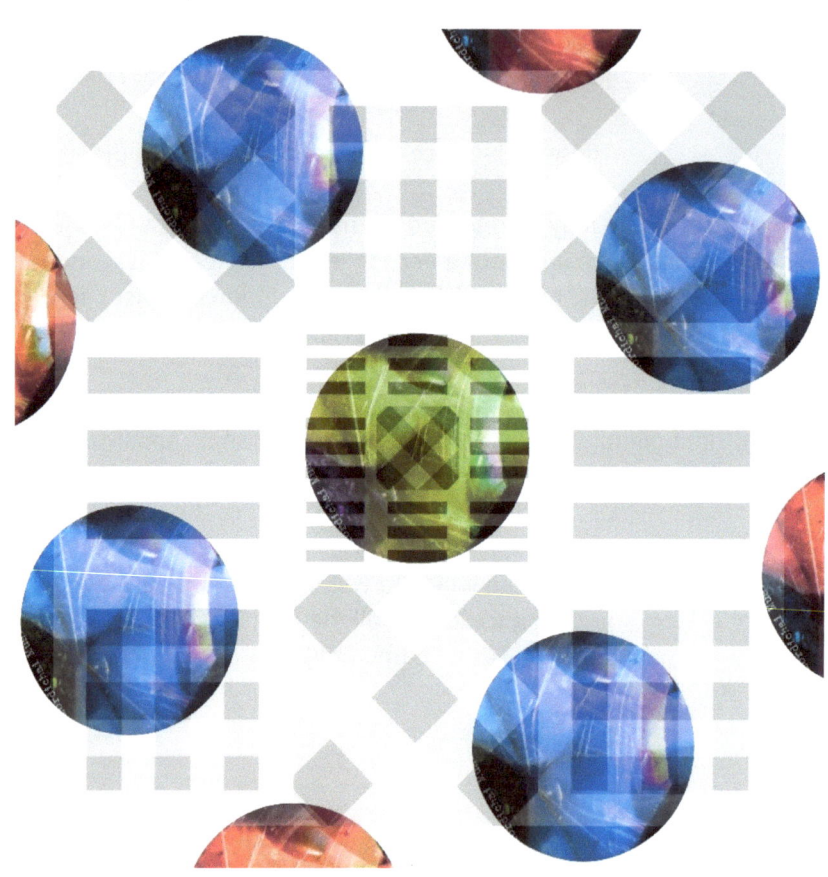

Another version of our beautiful mystery object.

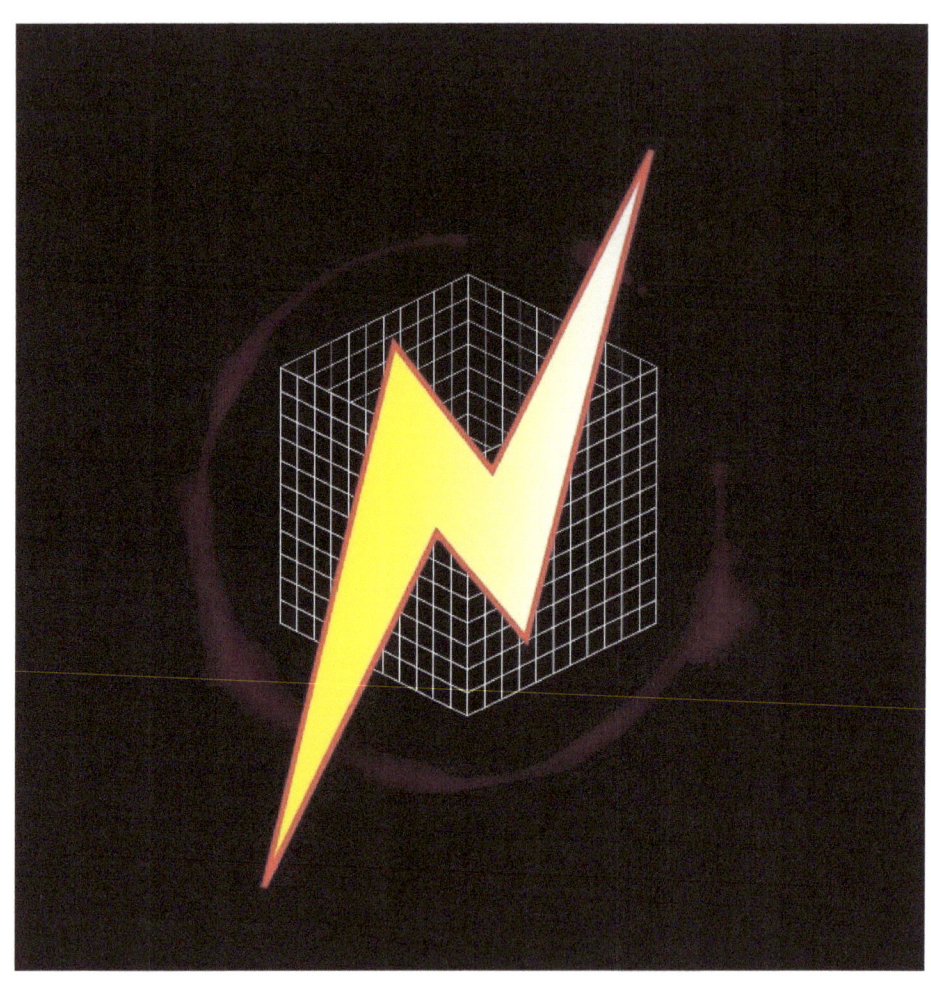

Sometimes lightning strikes in the studio and we all have wonderfully creative days and this may be exactly what it looks like from an outsider's perspective.

Of course some of us aren't quite all polished up.

With bands like Kryogenic, Dead Planet Society and aBSYNTh of dEATh…. Oh, we probably ought to include Vonnegut Sludge in there as well as a few you'll likely coming across if you visit our website.

All good though. This makes great wallpaper especially for those who wish to keep their screens longevity.

The artwork was definitely a part of our heavier side of the music genres.

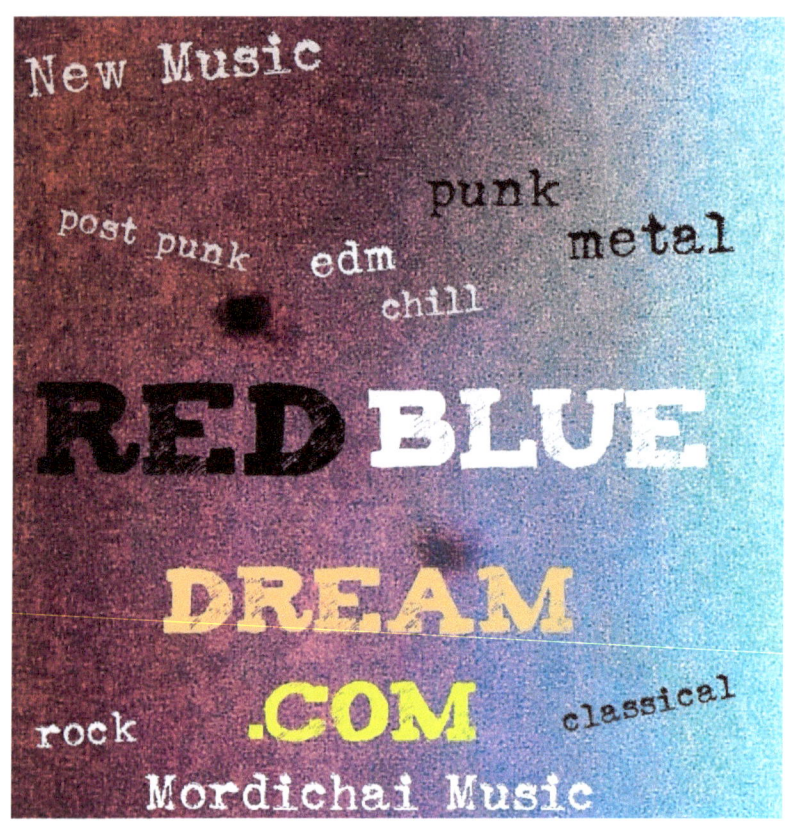

This is how that last photo had begun.

You see, sometimes things get really messed up around here and normalcy is actually more of an objective term than subjective and we just seem to go with the flow.

Morality is also superficial for many and subjective states of mind can skew the brain.

In this circumstance however we are just going to let this wonderfully ornate image speak for itself and let by gones, be by gones.

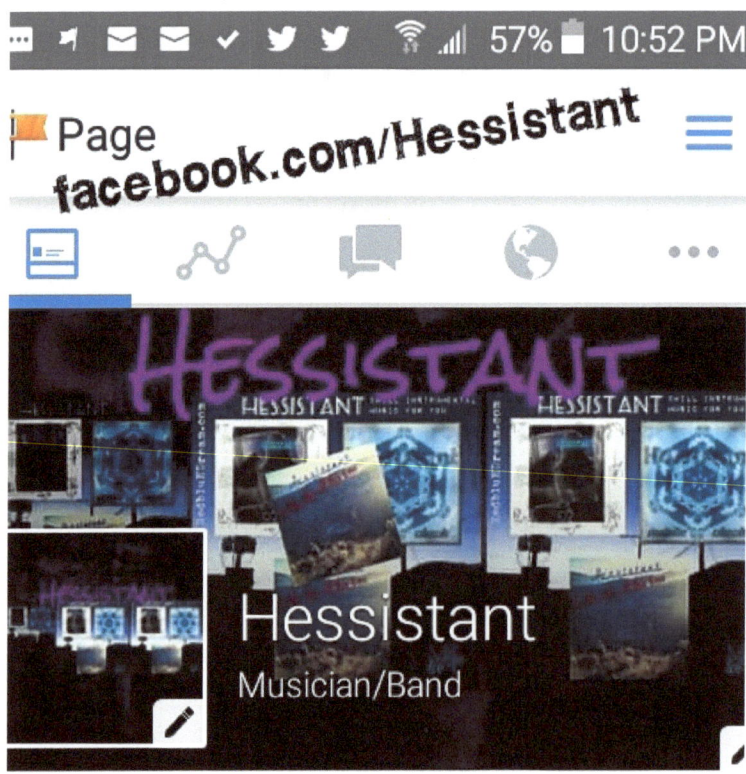

Okay we admit that we were showing off with this one.

This is our most beloved contemporary classical band Hessistant.

They simplify and ground our record label in a very nice way. Refinement is necessary when dealing with some of the clowns we deal with.

Veganism is a thing around here. For some reason we must insist you know.

No offence to the meat eaters either btw. We all have our thing.

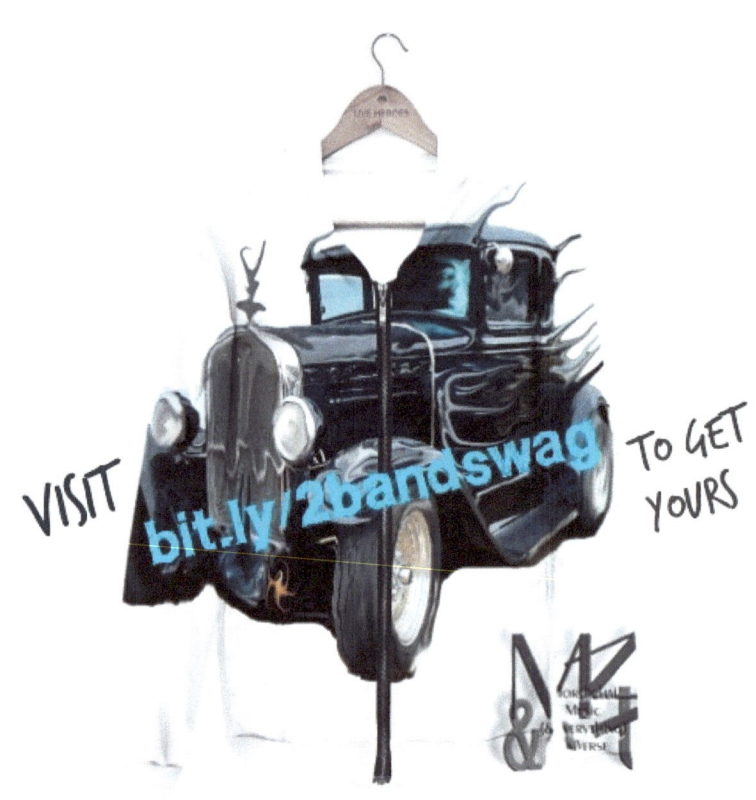

This was a shameless plug for our merchandise. We love out swag and sometimes even enjoy wearing it ourselves.

Old cars and stuff are our lovely little pleasure.

I personally took this photograph at an old car show and figured we just needed to have it on one of our wearables.

Okay so this isn't what it's cracked up to be at all. It started as a broken tree branch which appeared as a tetrahedron. It obviously wasn't, but we had to photograph it as such.

The stick was untouched as we passed it on the street. All we did was add some effects to the image.

Wear your heart on your sleeve.

OzkAn said it best in their song *Dragon Summary*. "Love is the answer, Love is the key."

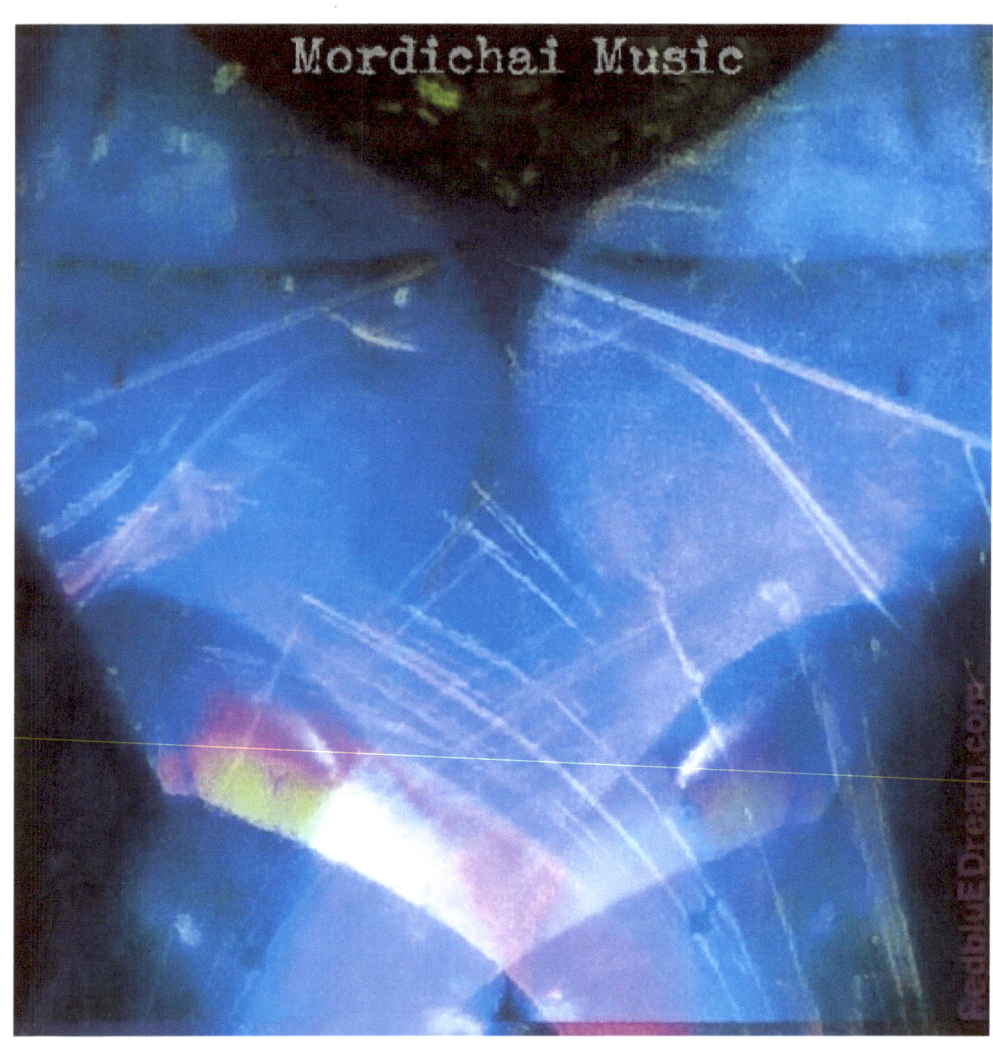

Remember the dots a few pages back?

This is a close up shot of our mystery object. Remember it has been altered from the original.

This is not the original color but something we had conceived in order to have one each of the primary colors and one each of the secondary.

Take note of the striations in the blue, perhaps an otherworldly images hidden within.

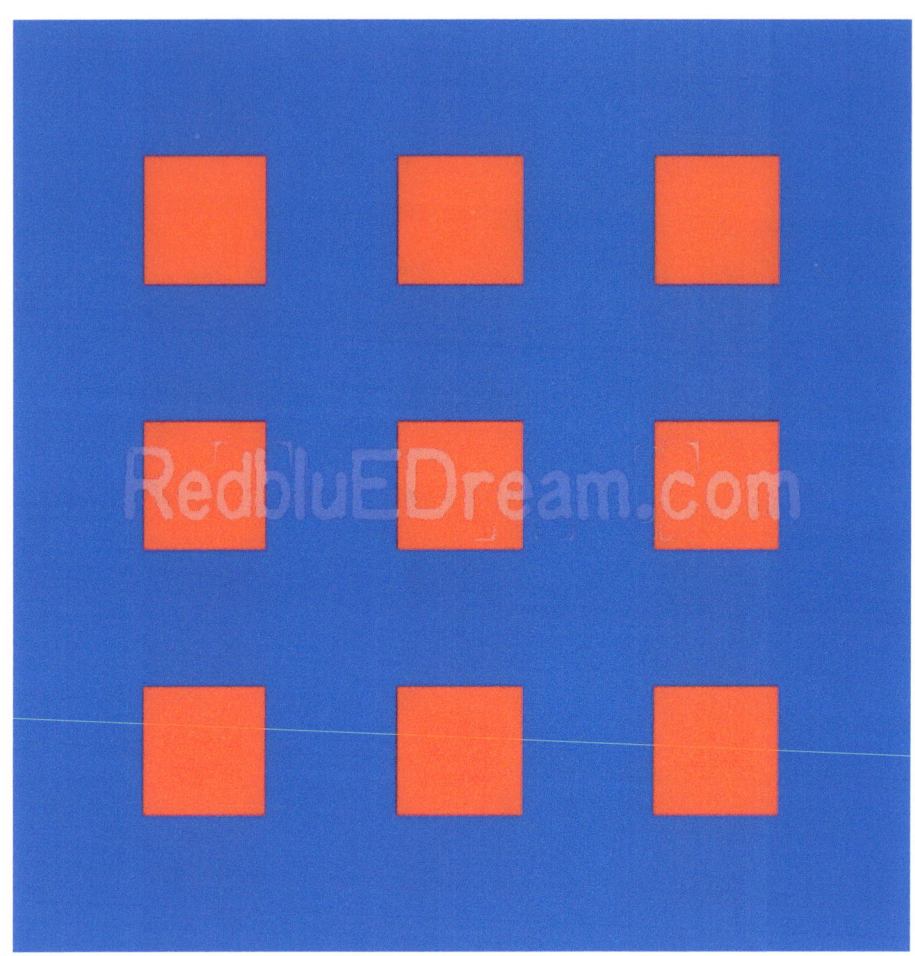

Shocking blue and nine red square pegs. Illusions may occur if you stare at it for a bit, especially the center square.

Not looking for Andy's approval on this one, but it does create a strange nostalgic tone which may softly echo inside one's cranium.

CHAPTER 5
Black & White

Life may not always be black and white, but when it is, the color certainly does stand out amazingly well.

We went on a bit of a black and white trip and wound up with some amazingly cool artwork. One of the more fun things about this segment, is that when you actually go to our Instagram account and view it on 'grid mode,' you can see the bigger picture.

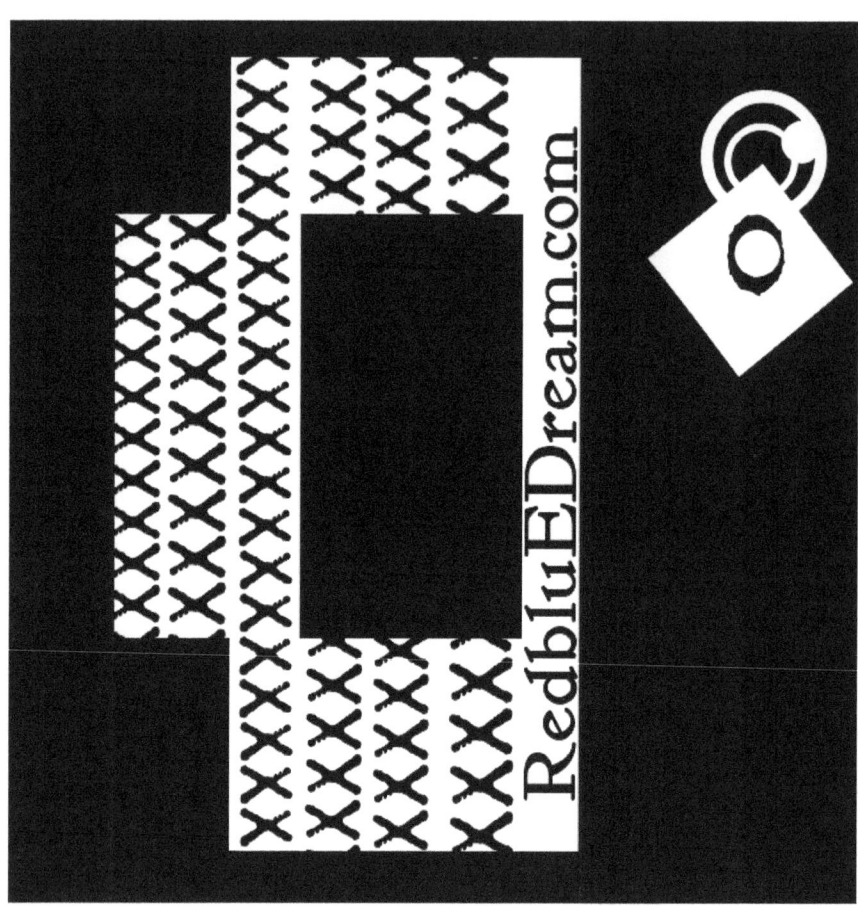

I did this one entirely on the phone with an app. It was inspired by not really wanting to post anything, yet needing to fulfill an obligation.

I used the multiple 'x' motif to in essence censor any content that may have appeared in the happy little white bits.

A figure '8' lurks in the top right corner, hiding the fact that it's a mask awaiting a ball.

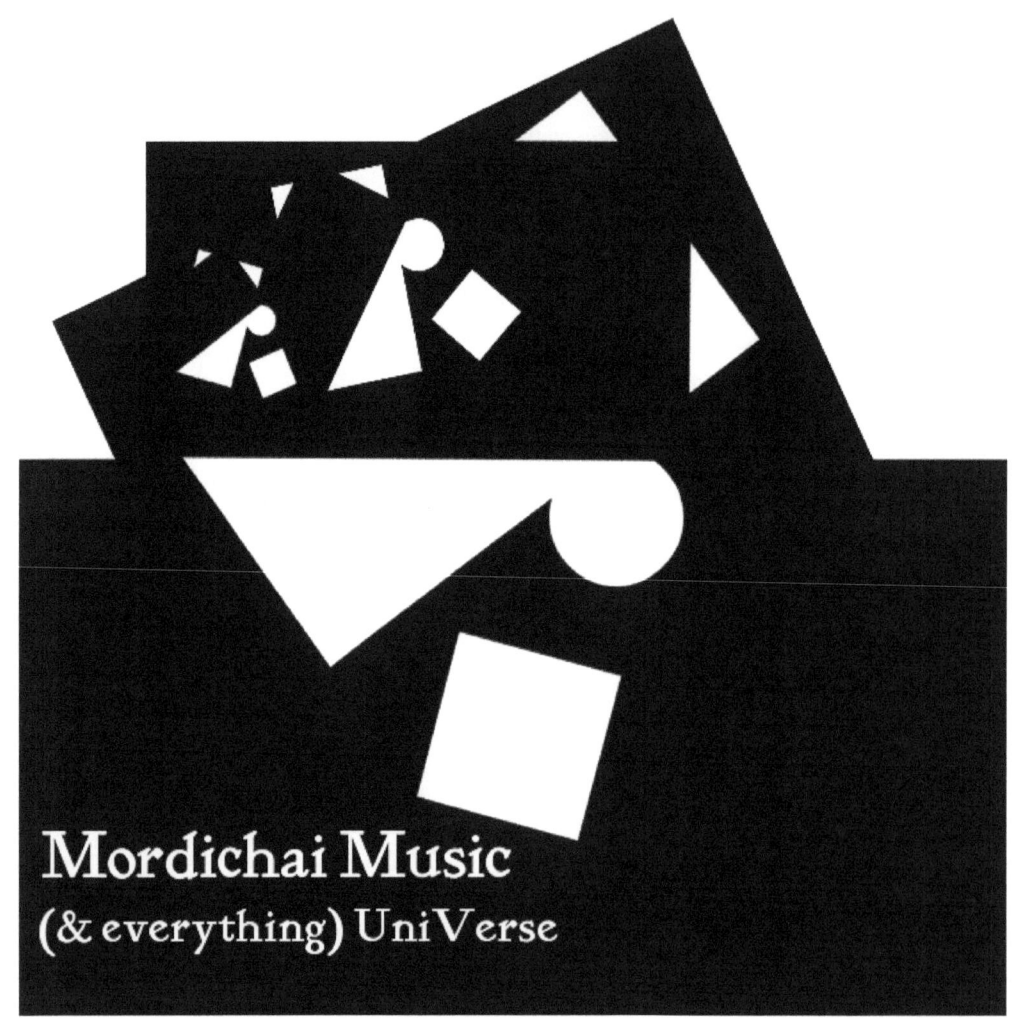

Mordichai Music
(& everything) UniVerse

This is an impressionistic impression of an impressionable man.

The motif began as a faux Mandelbrot set and evolved into this. Strange shapes, simply multiplied and angled, interacting in a weird freeform fashion.

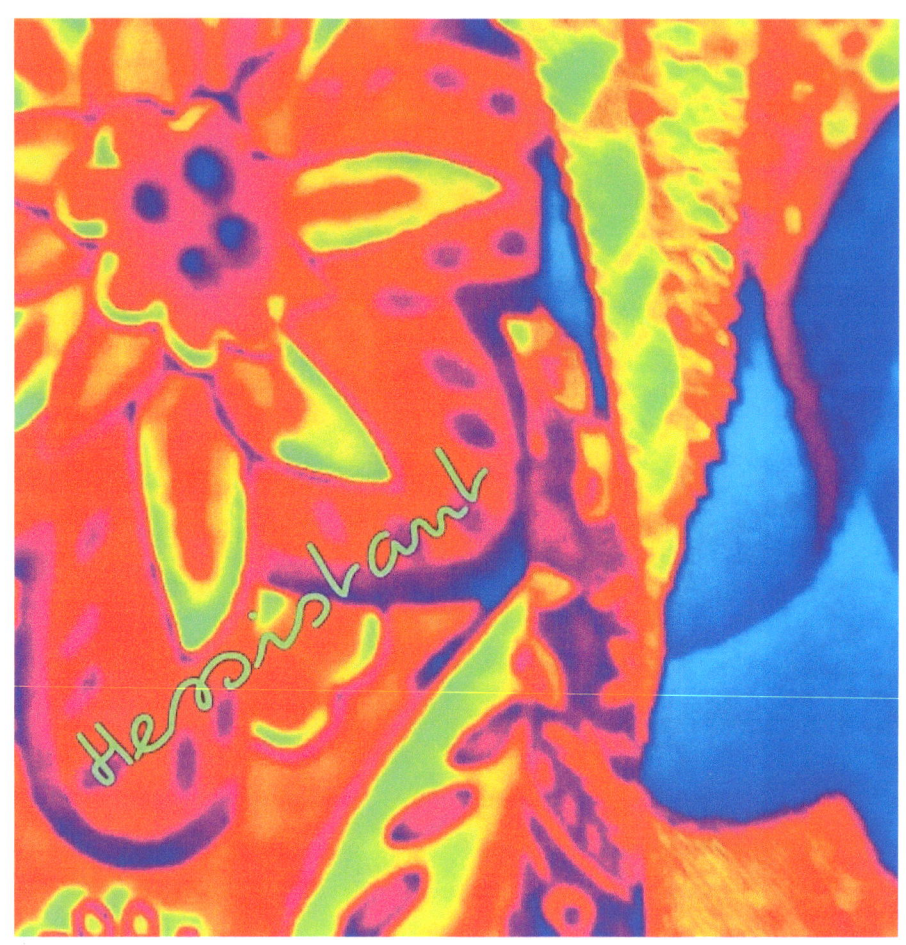

Bright colors, fantastic print. We couldn't resist but after photographing something so wonderful, the thought came to mind that maybe I could pull the colors out more with a filter, and one was applied giving it the 1960's feel I was looking for in this post for our contemporary and experimental classical project *Hessistant.*

We love the electric warmth and floral print. It makes us feel like the music of Hessistant.

MORDICHAI

CHAPTER 6
INTO THE VOID

We set ourselves into the void from time to time. Sometimes it is from our own doing and other times it is from situations brought upon us from circumstances that we had seldom ever expected to find ourselves in. No worries though, we usually pull through.

Being a multi-dimensional record label and entertainment company, Mordichai Music certainly isn't lacking as far as strange images go. In fact we practically thrive on such weirdness as it definitely seems to follow us around.

There isn't much else that we can say about this section, except "have fun."

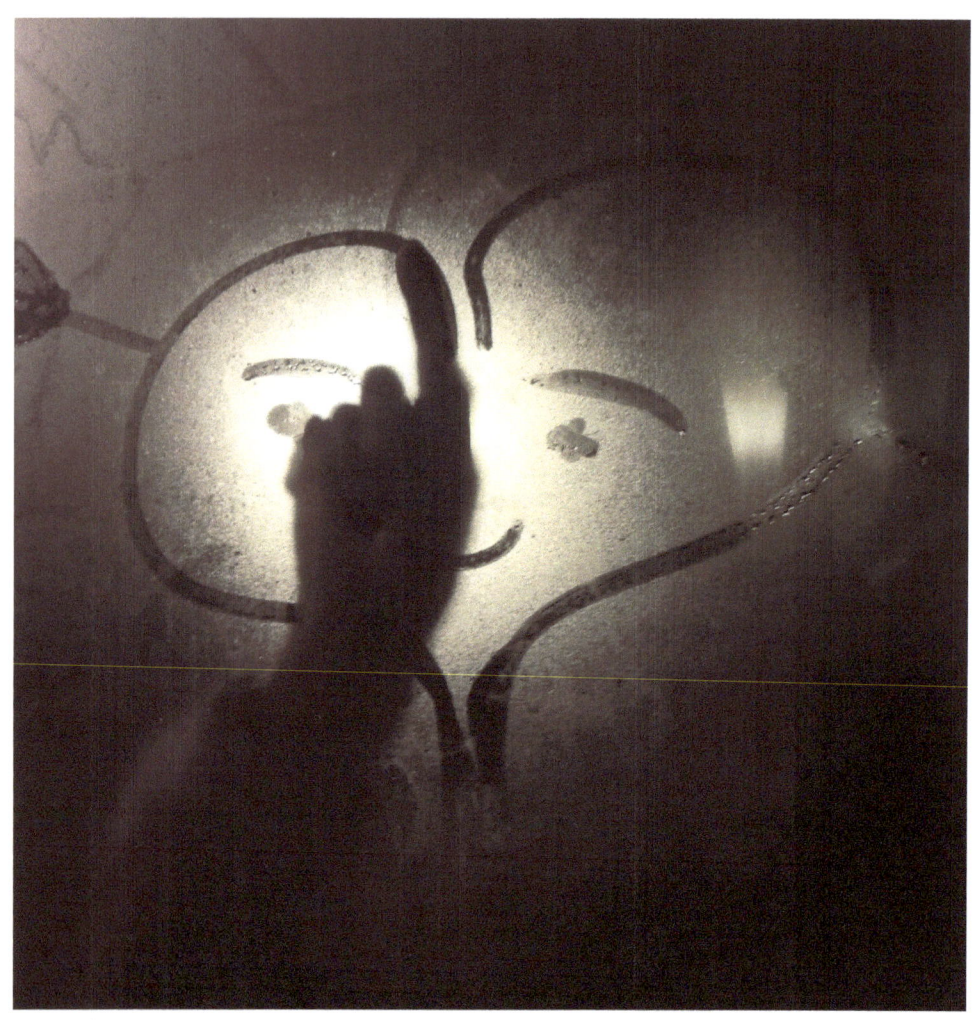

When Sister Mary sees an opportunity for providing temporary graffiti, she usually lets her creativity flow.
Her message is obvious and simple and you'd be surprised as to how easily it puts smiles on faces when they had seen it for the first time.

It is actually because of all the smiles we unexpectedly had around here with people seeing Sister Mary's handiwork on the window that lead me to capture this temporary art on a hard drive and share it with our social media

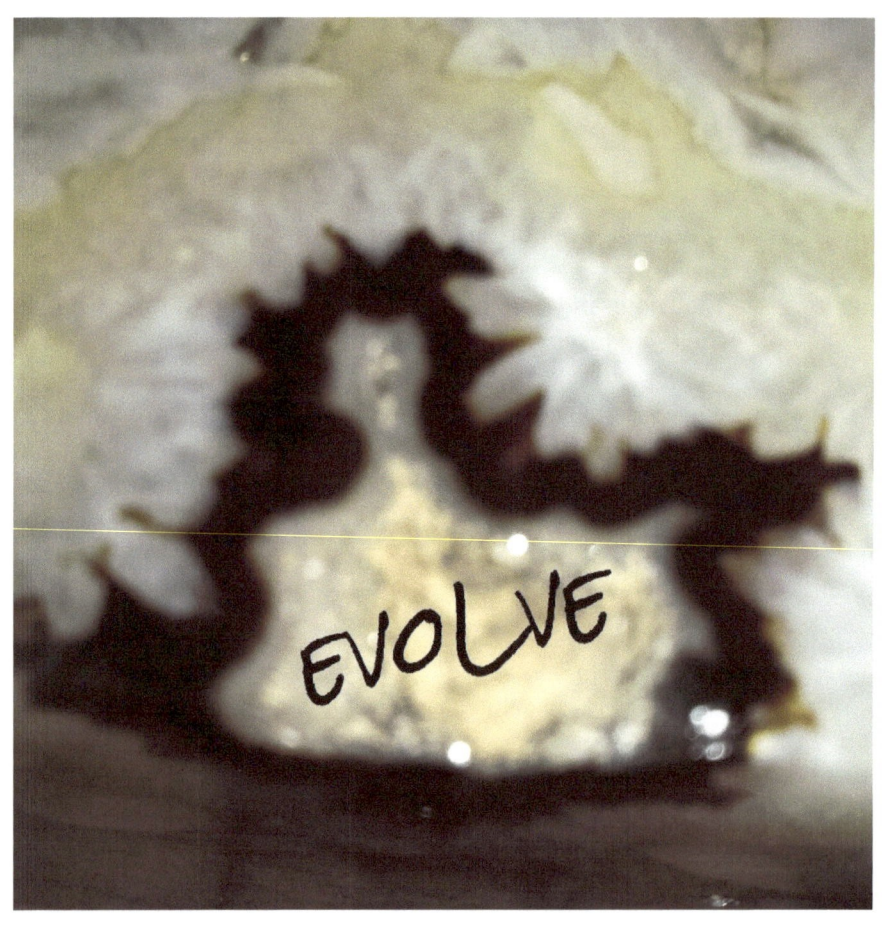

Can you guess what this is? Go ahead and have a better look before reading any further. I will wait.

Have you finished? If you said a chunk of quartz crystal you would be absolutely correct. I was playing with the camera one day and it was as if for the first time I had noticed the fine shapes and striations in the quartz.

The piece was given by a friend many years ago and makes its presence known from time to time as it catches the light. The friend on the other hand, has been missing for several years. Not to worry though, he will turn up when he wants to if he is still alive.

The word "evolve" boldly presents itself as the evolution of carbon is that which namely makes up quartz; silicon. Intense heat and pressure cause carbon to shine with a hardness and density and shimmer which humans love to decorate themselves with, so why not strive for a bright shiny future then?

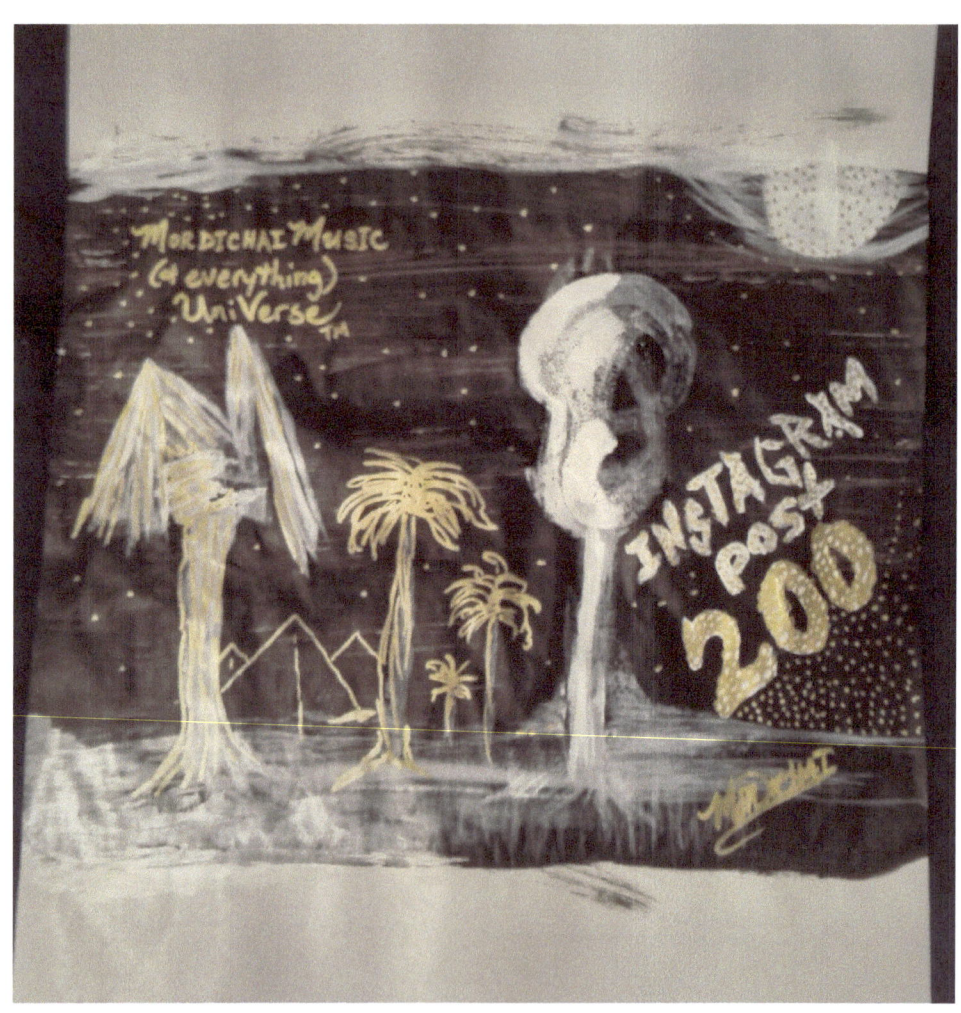

Post number 200 on Instagram. We needed to do something special for our 200th post, but not too special, you know. It was not like it was our 2000000th or anything. Still, the post deserved to be highlighted, so that is exactly what had occurred.

I am usually surrounded by art supplies and musical instruments and such so I decided to gather some paper and paints and this fancy gold pen we had laying around. I was not exactly certain as to what would be conveyed through the paint, but I did know it would be different from what I am accustomed to.

Palm trees and pyramids in the dark apparently emerged with joy and enthusiasm.

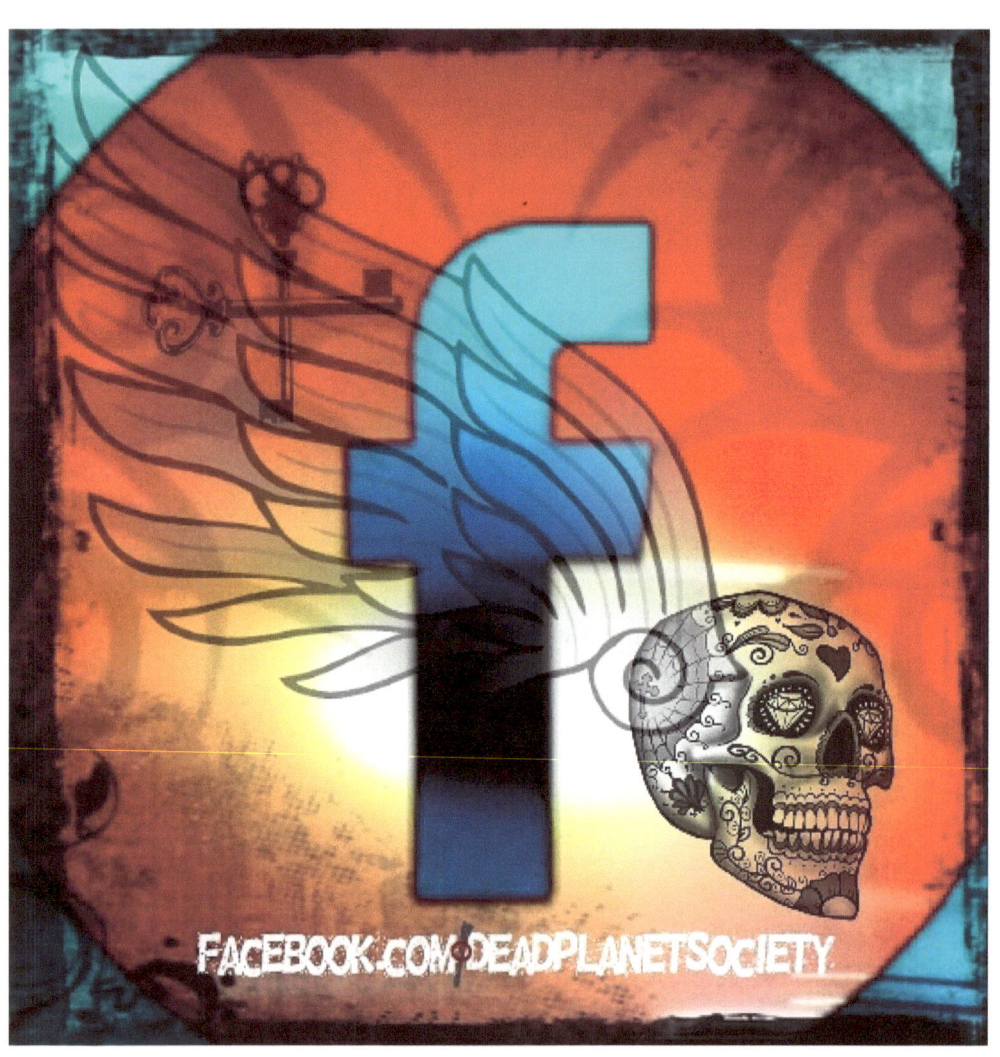

Many folks have a Facebook account. In fact, at the time of writing this there are about one billion Facebook accounts worldwide. We figured we would give our account wings.

Actually, we did one of these up for many of our bands and artists but you will just have to visit our Instagram account @MordichaiMusic.

The bold Red and Blue to congeal with the RedbluEDream.com website. Simple designs and ornate lines.

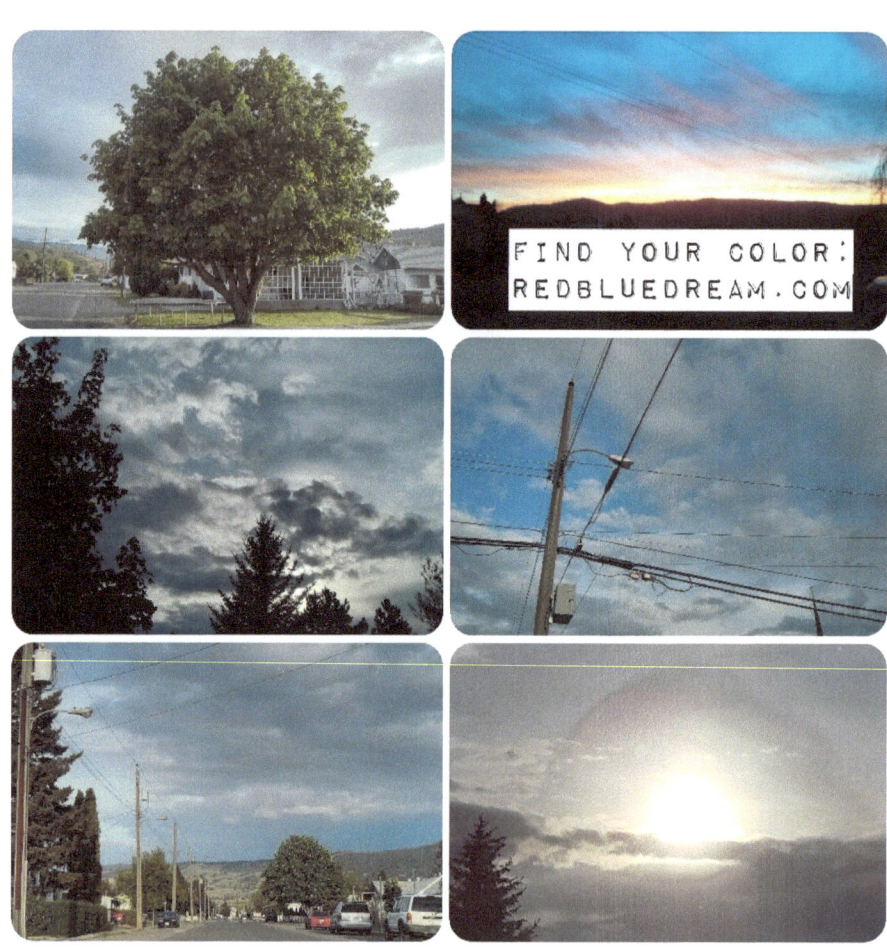

Six sky shots to behold.

It was a pleasure to both shoot and to put together this piece.

Top right reveals some extraordinary color coupled with the feathery, painted clouds of a setting sun. Even the blue is deeper than the rest of the photos.

There are a couple of themes intermingling in this series of photographs, yet each photo stands alone as well. It may also be interesting to know that these six photographs were shot within several blocks of a small town in British Columbia, over a span of about 2 years.

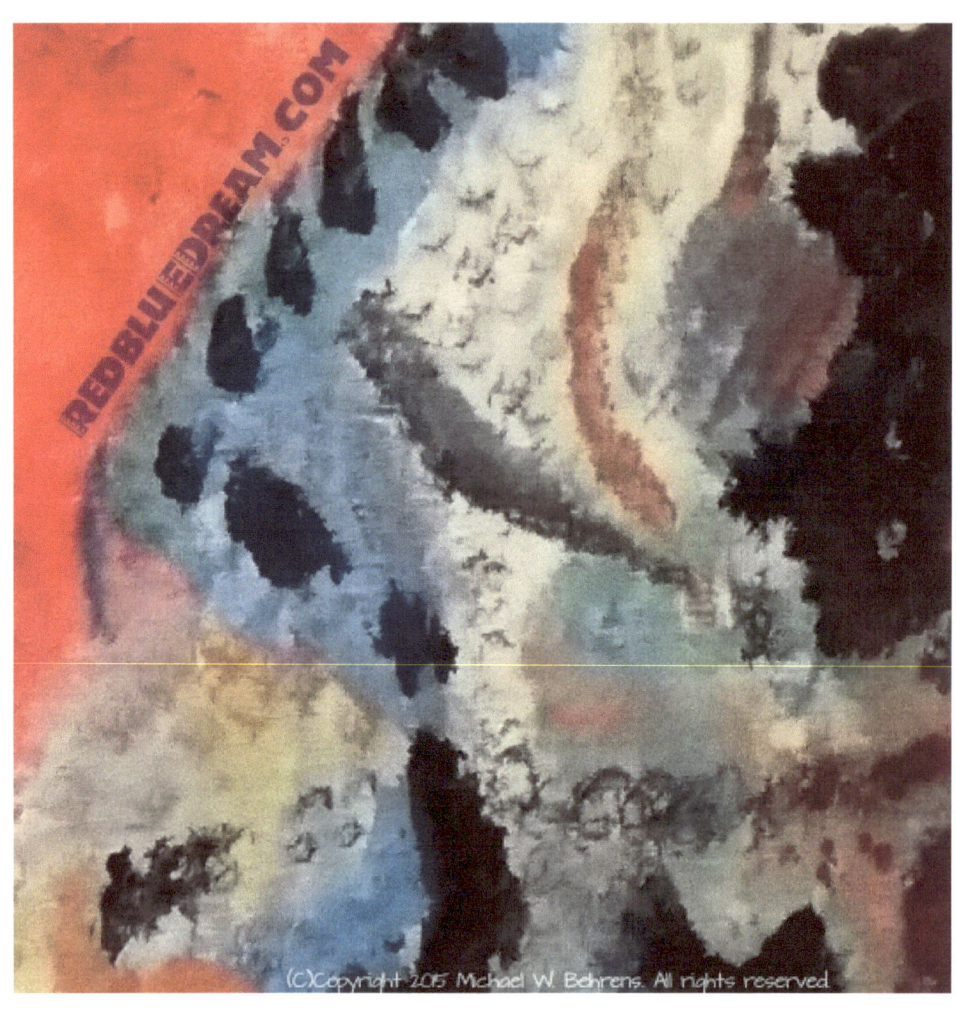

This is a small section of an oil painting called "The Heart of the Matter" that I had painted in 2008-2009. I painted it on our kitchen table rather than an easel. Seemed like a good idea at the time.

This abstract work was a gift for a friend and everyone who came into the house was warned of the wet paint.

Unfortunately, telling houseguests not to touch wet paint seemed futile as it appeared that pretty much everyone who walked through the kitchen, touched the wet paint. Even the recipient of the painting had gotten in on the fun and painted a section of their own.

High strangeness ensued shortly after the painting was complete. Quartz crystals seemed to spy on things throughout the crazy exploration of oil paint and discarded wood found at a site where a church was being converted to condominiums.

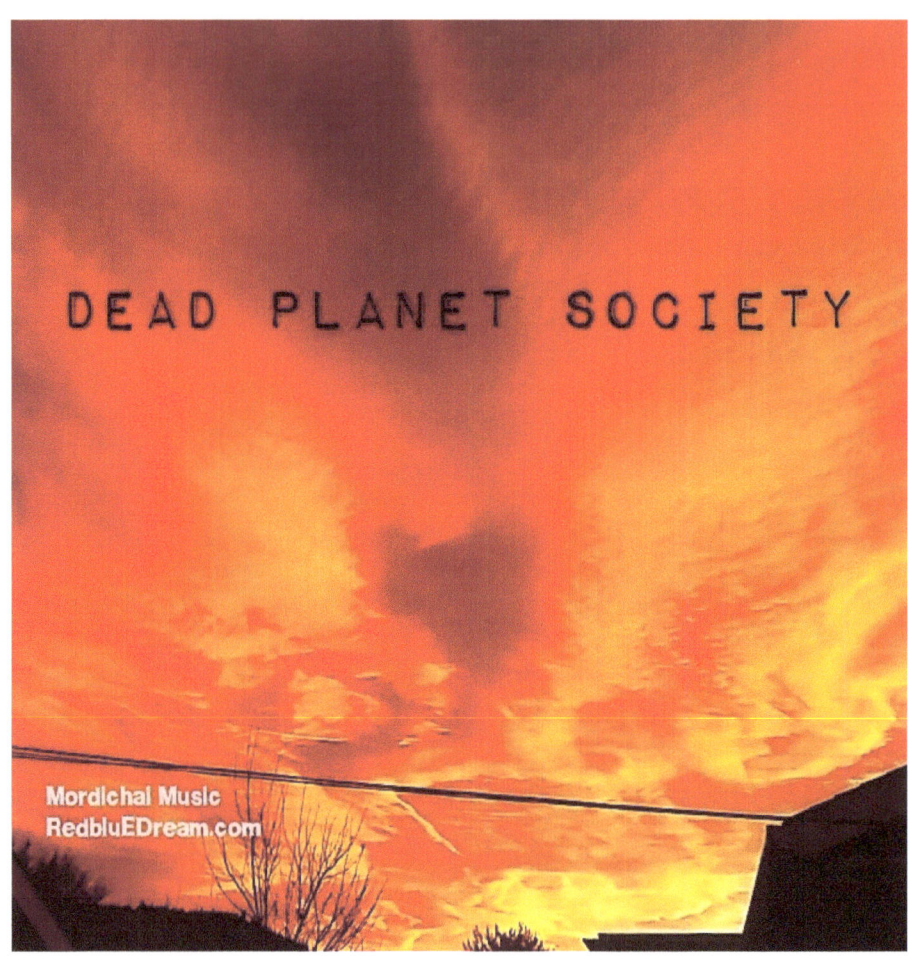

We just couldn't resist adding this beautiful augmented sunset photograph used for the nastiness known as Dead Planet Society.

The yellows and oranges just pop into your psyche and dominate you. The depth and richness of the tones exceed normal sunset expectations and suck you in to the images projected on the sky in that moment.

*** * ***

This photograph was taken in Merritt, British Columbia in the summertime.

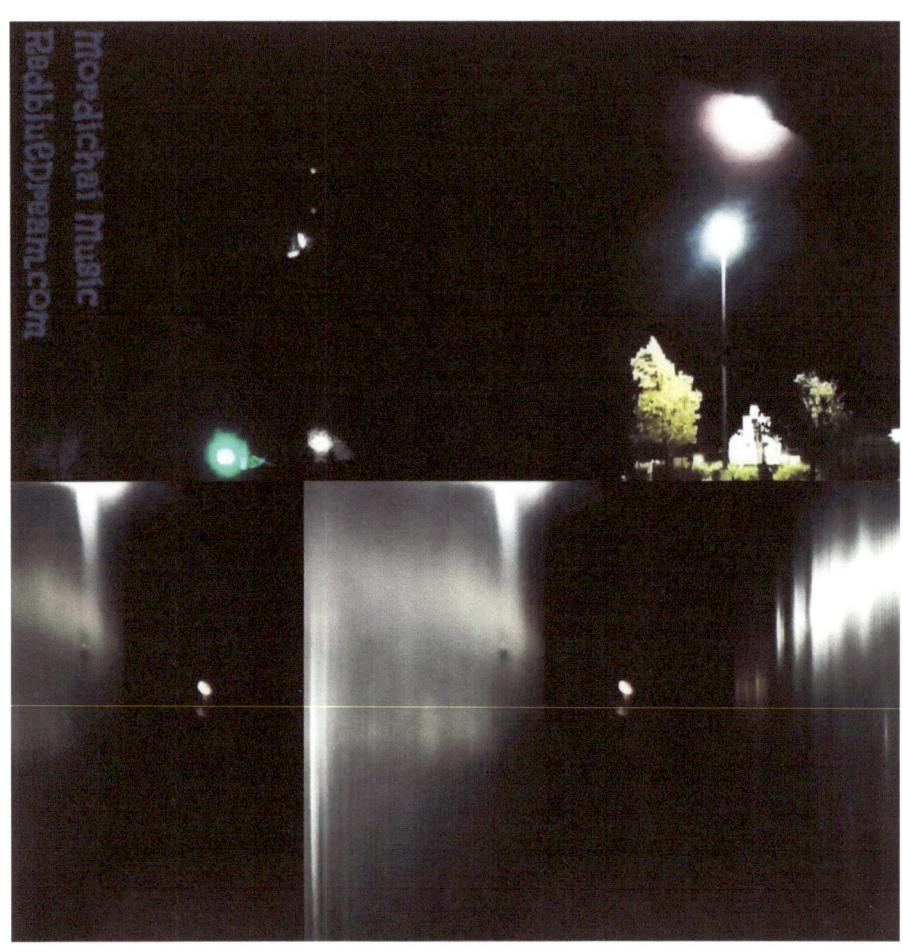

As the chapter's title "Into The Void" implies, we shall venture off into the void with this one. It's actually three or 2 ½ plus one.

The bottom section is a passageway used in many of our Mordichai Music pieces. One and ½ of the section used is an incredible passage which leads to sustenance, libations, knowledge and the unknown. Which is obviously why we love to use it for the works we had; including *"7 Tracks of Death The Musical,"* the film based on the music of aBSYNTh of dEATh.

Now the lights in the upper left corner were something else. Seemed like everywhere we went there were lights that evening. Winter. Coldness. Nonetheless we photographed mysterious things and lights that bring questions. You know how it goes.

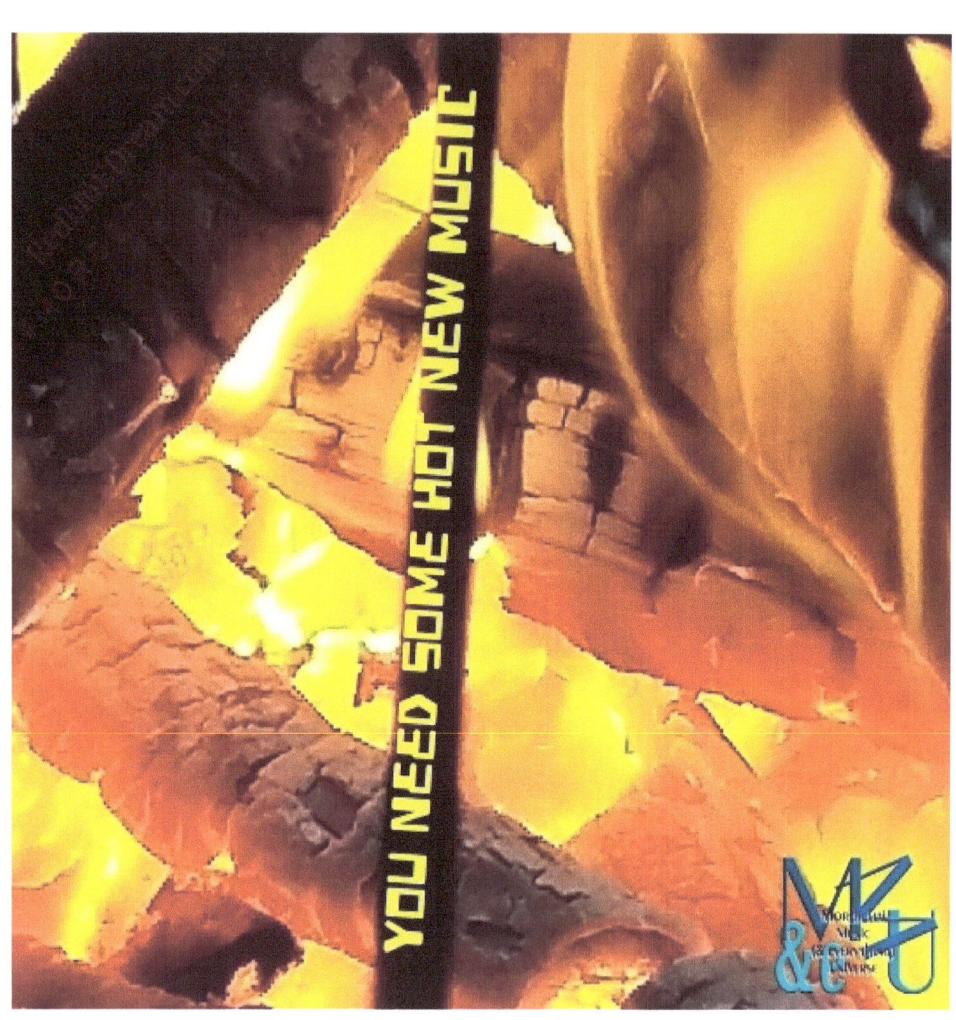

And all of this leads to this beautiful photograph from an impromptu family gathering which lead to this beautiful fire. We all took part in eating things cooked over the fire. Marshmallows included.

It was the incredible yellows once again which captured my attention and basically forced me into taking this moment into consideration as a viable candidate for immortality.

The burnt wood needs attention as well as we discover the beautiful lines and contrasts which reveal hidden images embossed in the flames and ash.

It was a beautiful evening and I suppose for me the best part of this image is that as awesome as it may be for you to see, I am one of few who know what had been in those moments as dusk set in.

ABOUT THE AUTHOR

Mordichai is an artist, musician, producer and more. Originally from the large metropolises of Ontario Canada, Mordichai now resides in the Cascade Mountains of British Columbia, Canada where he keeps his independent record label in motion as principal producer from punk / metal to classically influenced orchestration and edm tomfoolery.

MORDICHAI

www.ingramcontent.com/pod-product-compliance
Lightning Source LLC
Chambersburg PA
CBHW050717180526
45159CB00003B/1058